Karel & Ivan Kyncl

After the Spring Came Winter

**Translated from Czech
by George Theiner**

Askelin & Hägglund

CHARTA 77 FOUNDATION ● P.O. BOX 50041 ● S-104 05 STOCKHOLM ● SWEDEN

Published by the Charta 77 Foundation in Stockholm in
cooperation with and sponsored by:
Fritt Ord, Oslo, Norway
Help and Action, Paris, France
Index on Censorship, London, England
Informatie over Charta, Holland
International Committee for the Support of the Charta 77
in Czechoslovakia, Paris, France
Listy, Rome, Italy
Norwegian Helsinki Committee, Oslo, Norway
Stichting European Human Rights Foundation, London, England
Støttefondet før Charta 77, Skien, Norway
U.S. Helsinki Watch Committee, New York, NY, USA

Published in the United States under the auspices
of the U.S. Helsinki Watch Committe,
36 West 44th Street, New York, N.Y. 10036
(212) 840-9460

To Our Readers:

The book that you are holding in your hands is a special book, a very personal book. It is a book about human rights, with an emphasis on the word "human."

After the Spring Came Winter tells a story in words and pictures of a group of human rights activists, members of the Charter 77 movement in Czechoslovakia. People – those whose names usually appear as dry, legal statistics in reports on human rights repression – come to life in these pages: we see them engaged in their everyday world. We are shown their courage. We learn of their pleasures, as well as their problems, troubles and pain.

After the Spring Came Winter is the result of a close collaboration between father and son. Written by Karel Kyncl, a well known Czechoslovak journalist now living in London, it is illustrated with more than 100 photographs taken by his son Ivan. We find it haunting in its understatement, its lack of rhetoric. It adds a new dimension to human rights literature. A human one.

After the Spring Came Winter is dedicated to the exceptional people whose story it tells and to its readers. We hope that you will join us in the campaign to defend the rights of these persecuted citizens of Czechoslovakia.

František Janouch, The Charta 77 Foundation
Jeri Laber, U.S. Helsinki Watch Committee

Dear friends,

If this book arrives in your hands it will mean that both its authors have emigrated from Czechoslovakia. Or that they are in a Czech jail. *Tertium non datur.*

Below we reproduce the relevant paragraphs of the Czechoslovak Penal Code which we have infringed merely by publishing these photographs and the story of Charter 77:

§ **98 Subversion of the Republic**
§ **100 Incitement**
§ **112 Damaging the interests of the Republic abroad**

§ 98
Podvracení republiky

[¹] Kdo z nepřátelství k socialistickému společenskému a státnímu zřízení republiky provádí podvratnou činnost proti jejímu společenství, a státnímu zřízení, proti její územní celistvosti, obranyschopnosti nebo samostatnosti anebo proti jejím mezinárodním zájmům, bude potrestán odnětím svobody na jeden rok až pět let.

[²] Odnětím svobody na tři léta až deset let bude pachatel potrestán,

a) spáchá-li čin uvedený v odstavci 1 ve spojení s cizí mocí nebo s cizím činitelem,

b) spáchá-li takový čin ve větším rozsahu, nebo

c) spáchá-li takový čin za branné pohotovosti státu.

§ 100
Pobuřování

[¹] Kdo z nepřátelství k socialistickému společenskému a státnímu zřízení republiky nejméně dvě osoby pobuřuje

a) proti socialistickému společenskému a státnímu zřízení republiky,

b) proti její územní celistvosti, obranyschopnosti nebo samostatnosti, nebo

c) proti spojeneckým nebo přátelským vztahům republiky k jiným státům,

bude potrestán odnětím svobody na šest měsíců až tři léta.

[²] Stejně bude potrestán, kdo z nepřátelství k socialistickému společenskému a státnímu zřízení republiky umožní nebo usnadní šíření pobuřujícího projevu uvedeného v odstavci 1.

[³] Odnětím svobody na jeden rok až pět let bude pachatel potrestán,

a) spáchá-li čin uvedený v odstavci 1 tiskem, filmem, rozhlasem, televizí nebo jiným podobným účinným způsobem, nebo

b) spáchá-li čin uvedený v odstavci 1 nebo 2 za branné pohotovosti státu.

§ 112
Poškozování zájmů republiky v cizině

Československý občan nebo obyvatel republiky bez státní příslušnosti, který poškozuje zájmy republiky tím, že rozšiřuje nebo umožňuje rozšiřovat v cizině nepravdivou zprávu o poměrech v republice, bude potrestán odnětím svobody až na tři léta.

Words, words, words...

In Czechoslovakia under the Communist regime, it is the powers-that-be and not objective criteria that decide what constitutes "damaging the interests of the Republic abroad" or "subversion of the Republic", what is "hostility towards the socialist and state system", "independence", "allied and friendly relations", even what are "false reports".

Not exactly a new phenomenon — a leading representative of Nazi Germany once declared: "I decide who is and who is not a Jew."

However, undoctored photographs do not lie, and as far as the text is concerned, I have not written a single word which could not be borne out by unbiased witnesses or written documents.

There are several reasons why I did not find this an easy book to write.

A journalist who has been barred from exercising his profession for 11 years loses confidence. Especially when it comes to expressing himself. And even more so when the system under which he lives does not leave him in peace even in the unqualified job he is allowed to take and in his private life.

Apart from this, I had constantly to remind myself that I was writing for readers in the democratic world where, on the whole, the principles of logic do apply — and writing about events in a world where logic has been stood on its head. Writing about the kind of absurdity that can only be fully understood if you have lived in it as its

Hradčany (Prague Castle) once the residence of the Kings of Bohemia, today of the President of the Republic, Gustav Husák (View from Charles Bridge).

hostage. Without the possibility of leaving when you feel it has become too much for you. Without a passport, completely at its mercy. It is very difficult to try and convey this experience to readers who — fortunately for them — lack any adequate means of comparison. Many a time I had to go back to a typed page and add a sentence or two of explanation which would have been quite unnecessary had the book been intended for Czechoslovak readers. And I cannot be at all sure how far I have succeeded.

I felt a little like those American astronauts who walked on the Moon; they had film and TV cameras and microphones at their disposal, and later typewriters, and yet, as some of them have said in so many words, they could only convey a small fraction of their feelings and their experience to us mere groundlings. Well, Charter 77 is part of the moon landscape called Czechoslovakia. An indescribable landscape.

Also: this book came into being in Prague, both the photographs and the text. The photographs, which form its most important component, I mostly know only as negatives, and indeed so does the photographer. He sent many of them to friends abroad by various clandestine means as soon as he had exposed them, many of the snapshots he managed to save from the police during house searches, but preferred not to make any copies. It was easier to hide negatives than finished photographs. As for my text, I quickly stow it away whenever the front door bell rings, just in case...

We thus both have a pretty good idea what this book should look like, but only a very approximate one as to how it will actually appear when published. If it gets published at all, because we cannot be sure that the remaining negatives and pages of manuscript will make it safely across the Czechoslovak border, nor whether, having reached their destination, anyone in the West will be interested in such a book.

Finally, another considerable handicap was the fact that the photographs were taken by my son. I have had a far greater influence on his life than is usually the case with parents, for the Czechoslovak regime has its own ideas about "hereditary sin", which it takes to the most absurd lengths. A man who sins by discovering that the "revealed truth" of Communism which he once believed in is nothing but a lie and rejects it, pays a heavy price, and with him all his family. And not infrequently also his friends. (This is a feature of "real" socialism which I consider the most monstrous of all.)

In the first draft of this text I tried to ignore the father-son relationship between myself and the photographer. But then I realised that this was not possible. It seems to me that the circumstances under which this book came into being are no less telling in their documentary value than the photographs themselves. And perhaps they will help the reader "outside" understand the indescribable.

And so in the end I abandoned all pretence and have written about the author of the photographs with the same admiration I would have lavished on him had he been a complete stranger. If, nevertheless, I have not always succeeded in suppressing a father's pride, I ask the reader to forgive me. That is because I really *am* proud of my son.

Prague, May 1980
Karel Kyncl

Introducing
Czechoslovakia Today

August 1968: Statue of St Wenceslas in Wenceslas Square, Prague.

Prague is a city which, just forty years ago, seemed suddenly to switch from one continent to another. From Europe to Asia. Not in a literal, geographic sense, but geopolitically speaking.

This process took place within a mere decade, beginning with the earth tremors of Munich in 1938, through the volcanic eruption of the Second World War, to end in February 1948 with the final earthquake of the Communist coup.

It is perhaps because political terminology tends to be similar to the language of diplomats that the world still does not seem to have taken full cognisance of the change. In 1938 Czechoslovakia was still referred to as "the heart of Europe" and Prague "a Central European capital" — today, and for many years now, they belong, in political parlance, to "Eastern" Europe.

The geopolitical shift was accompanied by confusion in regard to the seasons of the year.

So it was that in 1968 the Prague spring started in January with its snow and frost, while the Prague winter came in the hot days of August.

At the time of the so-called international fraternal aid, given to Czechoslovakia by the armies of the Warsaw Pact, the author of the photographs in this book was only fifteen years old, and it was his mother who roamed the streets of Prague, camera in hand. He, in the meantime, was helping his fellow-countrymen put up protest posters and hated the foreign soldiers.

And, with the rest of the population, he imbibed the strange, marvellous, intoxicating atmosphere of solidarity and resistance to brute force and ignorance. He felt himself to be a tiny particle of an organism, functioning in harmony with all the other particles, atoms and molecules. His nation seemed to him like a top sportsman at the height of his career setting out to break the world record, confident that he can do it, that he can jump higher than anyone had done before him. That he can accomplish the seemingly impossible.

Not for one moment did he think that he might fail, that the sportsman might break an arm or a leg. Or indeed his neck.

Indignantly he rejected his mother's suggestion that she take a snap of him underneath an inscription, scrawled in huge black letters on a Prague wall:

IVAN, GO HOME!

And in all seriousness he considered changing his Christian name.

Then the record attempt failed and the sportsman limped back to the dressing-room to lick his wounds. The shock of failure triggered all the infirmities that had hiterto lain dormant in his body. He turned into an invalid riddled with rheumatic pain, varicose veins and a heart ailment, and he began to think that it is much easier to crawl under an obstacle than jump over it. Our hero slowly conformed to the changed situation. Only now and again, when he has put away a few pints of Pilsener, does he feel a twinge of the old ardour, of his old ambition to achieve the impossible. But before he gives any sign of it,

A Prague street in August 1968. In the middle, Ivan Kyncl.

Prague in August 1968.

he takes a careful look around him, to make sure it is safe to do so. To make sure that the heretical remark he is about to utter will not cause an inconspicuous-looking gentleman at the next table to rise from his chair, wave a piece of ID in his face, and take him straight to the nearest police station...

But enough of metaphors. Useful as they are, they have their limits.

Unlike the fifteen-year-old in 1968, today Ivan Kyncl knows that a nation is not composed of atoms and molecules but of individuals, who will act in almost complete unison only on very rare

occasions, usually in the most dramatic moments of their nation's history. At other times — and history consists largely of those *other* times — each individual behaves differently, does his own thing, reacting to his surroundings and to world-shaking events according to his own lights, his own character, and the influences which shaped or deformed him. "Will of the people", "the national character", "proletarians of the world",

The "liberators" taking a look round the "liberated" city: Soviet soldiers in Prague.

There is little fraternisation between the Soviet officers and the population, and that is why...
...unusual street signs have had to make their appearance in the streets of Prague — in the Russian alphabet.

10

"we Czechs", "we British", "we Soviet people" — all these are nothing but empty, nonsensical labels, shorthand characters which conceal a whole multitude of different, and frequently contradictory, meanings.

Today Ivan is 27, and he has long ago come to terms with the knowledge that he will go through life with that Christian name which his parents, in their naïve idealism, gave him all those years ago. What he has not come to terms with, though, is the "real Socialism" which has become reality in his homeland.

While he was still living there, he got into the habit of walking the streets of the capital and looking at the city through the viewfinder on his camera.

Prague is a truly beautiful city, its thoroughfares, parks, gardens and palaces containing countless poetic nooks, panoramas and scenes. However, the Prague Winter does not favour poetry.

The baroque palaces and churches, the castle of Hradčany and the patrician houses, the narrow lanes of the Old Town and the Little Quarter — all these are today a mere backdrop for something that used to give them life but that is no longer there.

Quite different buildings have come to play an increasingly important role in the life of the city and its inhabitants:

The Ministry of the Interior of the Czechoslovak Socialist Republic. The headquarters of the Communist state's most powerful institution.

You may find it surprising that the most powerful institution is not the Central Committee of the Communist Party; true, the Communist Party plays a leading role in

The Ministry of the Interior.

A view across the prison wall: Pankrác Prison in Prague.

The Supreme Court and the offices of the Czechoslovak Procurator General.

Czechoslovakia, but State Security, in turn, plays a leading role in the Party.

And State Security — StB — is the most important part of the Ministry of the Interior.

Prisons.

One of many in Czechoslovakia, this is Prague's most notorious prison at Pankrác, where the Nazis beheaded their opponents. And where, in the 1950s, the Communists treated the same kind of people to a more humane method of execution than the axe. The noose.

Today, a political prisoner will probably only get here if he falls ill with a complaint that pills cannot cure. In that case he will be put in handcuffs and transported to Pankrác, because this prison happens to have a sick bay and a hospital. A very primitive hospital, nevertheless

one in which minor operations can be carried out. On prisoners.

No, what am I saying: *on prisoners?*

Hardly. For in Czechoslovakia there are no "prisoners", only "convicted persons". And there are certainly no "political prisoners". In this respect, official propaganda is absolutely right: the Czechoslovak penal code knows no such category. There are simply no "political crimes" in Czechoslovakia. Ergo — anyone convicted in the courts is a criminal, pure and simple, whether guilty of murder or of holding non-conformist views. Similarly, there are no jails or prisons, only "institutions of correctional education". Nor is there any "police", only "security".

Calling a Czech policeman a "policeman" can be considered an offence, or — as the penal code puts it — "an attack on a public official". For this you can get three years in jail (sorry, three years' "loss of liberty").

This idea that giving something that is unpopular a different name will stop it being unpopular is by no means a Czechoslovak speciality. Rather, it is a Communist phenomenon.

Remember George Orwell's *Nineteen-Eighty-four*?

The Ministry of War in that book is called Ministry of Peace.

The ministry where history is being rewritten is called the Ministry of Truth.

And the ministry where the secret political police imprisons and tortures its victims is called Ministry of Love.

Right next to the Pankrác "institution of

two institutions in separate buildings when they enjoy such close cooperation?

And from here the "convicted person" can comfortably reach his cell in a matter of minutes, by way of an underground passage. All it takes is for the Supreme Court, as the court of appeal, to accede to the General Prosecutor's proposal and confirm the verdict.

The Supreme Court is there to confirm or increase the sentence passed earlier by some other court. In Prague it is usually here:

The young woman standing in front of the Municipal Court building is Anna Šabatová. The photograph was taken shortly before the opening of the trial of six members of the Czechoslovak Committee to Defend the Unjustly Prosecuted (VONS) at the end of October 1979. Or, as

Anna Šabatová in front of the Prague Municipal Court.

correctional education" stands one of the buildings of the Ministry of Love. Huddling cosily under one roof we find here the Czechoslovak Supreme Court and the General Prosecutor's Office of the Czechoslovak Socialist Republic. Of course, why bother to place these

judicial jargon would have it, proceedings "against Petr Uhl & Co." Anna Šabatová-Uhlová who, as the wife of the chief accused, was allowed to be present in court, was forcibly ejected on the first day of the trial. She had insisted on her right to take notes during the hearing.

The relatives of members of VONS (Committee for the Defence of the Unjustly Prosecuted) in front of the court building.

It was in this way that she — at last — became personally acquainted with this seat of socialist legality for Prague and the Central Bohemian Region.

With socialist legality itself she was acquainted already. In 1972, the Regional Court in Brno sentenced her to three and a half years in prison. She was released, conditionally, after two.

That same year, a brother of hers received an unconditional and another a conditional sentence.

Her father, Professor Jaroslav Šabata, was sent to prison in 1972 for six and a half years, being conditionally released five years later. A Charter 77 spokesman, he was re-arrested in October 1978 and sentenced to nine months' imprisonment, plus the 18 months that remained of his previous term.

And finally, Anna's husband, Petr Uhl, had already served a full four years from December 1969 to December 1973 and now, in October 1979, he was again in the dock of the Prague Regional Court.

A commonplace family snapshot?

Well, yes and no.

Members of four families met outside the Prague Regional Court: the Bednářs, the Uhls, the Bendas and the Němecs.

The families of four of the six accused in the VONS trial, who a week later were to receive the following sentences:

Otta Bednářová: three years.

Petr Uhl: five years in the second (more severe) penal category.

Dr Václav Benda, a Charter 77 spokesman: four years.

Dr Dana Němcová: two years, conditional.

The other two, the playwright Václav Havel and the journalist Jiří Dienstbier, another Charter spokesman, were sent to prison for four and a half years and three years respectively.

They were the first of the ten Charter signatories and VONS members to be imprisoned, ten people whose case aroused interest throughout the world.

And in Czechoslovakia.

I deliberately stress in Czechoslovakia, because as far as information about what goes on in his country is concerned, the Czechoslovak citizen is living in the pre-Guttenberg era, only slightly modernised by the existence of typewriters and cameras. The official news media are not there to provide information but rather to "educate the working people in the spirit of socialism". And so people have to rely for their real news on oral communication, with all its disadvantages — lack of accuracy, fragmentary nature of the information, and the ever-present possibility of distortion. Disadvantages to some extent offset by the Czech and Slovak transmissions on western radio stations, a wide range of samizdat publications of all kinds — which are more factual and authentic but whose numbers are of course limited by the number of copies produced by a typewriter — and, in the case of the ten VONS accused, photographs.

Several hundred and perhaps even thousand copies of this picture went the rounds in Czechoslovakia shortly after the arrest of the VONS members in May 1979. They were to become a valuable document — and one of the objects most frequently confiscated by Czechoslovak State Security during house searches.

Neither the indictment nor the verdict took much trouble in defining the "crimes" which the accused are supposed to have committed: VONS was alleged to be an anti-State organisation, the VONS press releases dealing with victims of political persecution "slandered the Republic",

The 10 arrested VONS members: Václav Havel, Otta Bednářová, Petr Uhl, Jarmila Bělíková, Jiří Němec, Ladislav Lis, Jiří Dienstbier, Dana Němcová, Václav Benda, Václav Malý.

In front of the Prague Municipal Court at the time of the VONS trial.

16

all VONS members had acted out of "hostility to the socialist system" and had been guilty of "subversive activity".

Equally anti-State, subversive and hostile was apparently the endeavour of several hundred people to attend the VONS trial, despite the fact that it was officially described as "public".

What that means, where the Czechoslovak penal system is concerned, was also experienced at first hand by many foreign witnesses — journalists, embassy officials, and the representatives of Amnesty International and other, similar organisations. Not a single one managed to get inside the courtroom.

During the two days of the trial, there was effectively martial law in force outside the Municipal Court buildings. The pictures on the next few pages were taken on the first day — when the police behaved with greater restraint

Psychologist Dr Dana Němcová the day she was conditionally released. (In the first picture with Anna Šabatová, wife of Petr Uhl, sentenced in the same trial to five years' imprisonment.)

In front of the Supreme Court on the day of the appeal hearing of the VONS members.

than on the following day, and when those who wanted to enter the building were merely pushed on to the opposite pavement and only some twenty people were arrested. Ivan Kyncl took the pictures with one hand while hanging on to the steering-wheel of his car with the other.

On the second day of the trial, you would be arrested simply for walking along the pavement past the court buildings, even if you did nothing, called out no slogans and carried no banner.

A logical conclusion to these pictures (and also a conditionally optimistic one) is provided by

Prague street

photographs which might by captioned "First Day of Freedom".

Because of her ill health, Dana Němcová, sentenced to two years' imprisonment, was conditionally released and able to return home.

Then came 20 December 1979. The first snow of the year fell in Prague, and the VONS members' appeals were heard by the Supreme Court in the building which it shares with the General Prosecutor's Office.

Again, no surprises: all the verdicts were confirmed by the court of appeal, and apart from a handful of the closest relatives no one was allowed to attend the hearing.

And yet, State Security did provide an original touch: they arrested a number of people who wished to attend the trial, six of whom they did not release in Prague but drove to a remote part of East Bohemia, near Žehušice, in six cars, leaving them to make their own way home across the snowy woods and fields in the middle of the night. Naturally, the detained people were released singly, to rub in the message that they were isolated, helpless, and at the mercy of the all-

powerful state.

So much for the Helsinki Accords.

And while the chief judge at the appeal hearing, Dr Marie Dojčárová, presided over the non-public "public" proceedings —

while StB officers were dispersing the small crowd outside the building —

while the Prague Ministry of the Interior, in collaboration with the Ministry of Foreign Affairs, was drawing up papers announcing the expulsion of Amnesty representatives, an official French delegation, and observers sent by the Association of Democratic Lawyers from the country —

while the StB drivers were filling up their cars with expensive petrol for the long journey to Žehušice —

— the vast majority of Prague's inhabitants went about their daily business. They stood in queues for meat, drank in pubs during working hours, were being bored out of their minds at the all-too-frequent Party and trade union meetings (also held during working hours), and some perhaps actually working. None of them had any

idea of what was happening. And it is highly unlikely that, had they known, they would have done anything about it. Nevertheless, the regime left nothing to chance, bringing in sizeable reinforcements of police from outside the capital. Just in case.

But, of course, nothing happened.

It was just another dull, ordinary day in the eleventh year of the Prague Winter.

Czechoslovak citizens have learned to pass by all these banners and slogans without taking them in. Only rarely now will someone find the inflated and mendacious propaganda so objectionable as to risk tearing it down on the sly.

I have read somewhere that in New York, water consumption rises sharply when TV commercials are shown because viewers use these times to visit the lavatory. No such statistics are available in Prague, nor can they be. Even if Czechoslovakia had a Public Opinion Research Institute (which it no longer has, as it was abolished as "unnecessary" following the Soviet invasion). Commercials for "real socialism", internationalism, and all the other isms don't just fill in the intervals between programmes — they *are* the programme.

There are other differences between this sort of propaganda and American TV commercials. Not only are the Prague commercials blatantly untruthful and lacking in inventiveness (at least on the artistic side), but any criticism of the State's propaganda, not to mention actual damage done to it, qualifies as a criminal offence.

Yet, something new and different did make its appearance among all these ubiquitous slogans.

And again the beautiful city of Prague got its seasons confused, for these signs of a burgeoning new spring appeared in January.

January 1977.

It was then that 240 Czechoslovak citizens signed Charter 77, men and women of very diverse political and religious views. The Charter did not call for anything particularly dramatic. It merely appealed to the government and to Czechoslovakia's leading representatives to adhere to the laws they had themselves promulgated, ratified, approved and signed — and they offered their assistance in doing so.

While the document itself was restrained enough, it did produce a dramatic effect.

The authorities reacted by arresting and interrogating the signatories, who were subjected to every conceivable kind of harassment, followed by secret police at every step, dismissed from their jobs, denounced in the press, on radio and TV (all these of course being in official hands) as "counter-revolutionaries", dissidents, "right-wing opportunists" ... Public meetings were called to express "the people's disagreement and condemnation", and dirty tricks of the pettiest kind were perpetrated against those who had dared to put their signature to Charter 77.

"Counter-revolutionaries" — "dissidents" — "right-wing opportunists". Again just words, words, words, to quote Hamlet.

Prague streets in 1977.

A counter-revolutionary is someone who opposes a revolutionary process. But what is a revolutionary process? Can one seriously use this term to describe a system holding the vast majority of its people in thrall by means of the police, informers and bureaucrats?

A dissident is someone who disagrees with the *status quo* and tries, by legal means, to bring about a change. So you might say that a British citizen who wants to abolish the House of Lords because he considers it to be an out-dated institution was a dissident. But why put that label on someone who is simply asking that his government respect its own laws?

As for a right-wing opportunist, that is a quite nonsensical piece of terminology. There is as much confusion in Czechoslovakia about "right-wing" and "left-wing" as there is about the year's seasons. And an opportunist, the dictionary tells us, is someone who does "what is opportune at the time, or expedient", someone who, regardless of principles, conforms to a given situation.

By the middle of 1980, over a thousand people had signed the Charter, not just in Prague but all over the country. This despite the fact that the movement has no firm organisational structure — an impossibility in a police state such as Czechoslovakia today — making regular contact between the signatories extremely difficult. As a result, the information available to them can at best only be fragmentary and incomplete. It is also impossible for one man with a camera to provide a photographic record of all those courageous men and women.

He thus had to do the best he could.

And even that took a great deal of courage.

Not infrequently did the photographer experience fear when he pressed the release of his camera. In the case of some of the pictures in this book, it is quite obvious why this should have been so; looking at some of the other photographs you may wonder why their quality should be inferior to those you are used to seeing in your magazines. Taking those pictures, Ivan Kyncl was

not always able to prevent his hands from shaking, and it is this unusual circumstance, as well as his prowess as a photographer, that must take the blame.

But we should not forget that the chief culprit is the Czechoslovak secret police.

24

The Charter People

This picture of a grave at the start of a chapter on the people who signed Charter 77 is not, I assure the reader, a cheap attempt to appeal to his emotions.

The story behind that grave is too serious for that.

Professor Jan Patočka was a philosopher — an idealistic philosopher, which in present-day Czechoslovakia is used as a derogatory term. The *Shorter Philosophical Dictionary*, published in Prague in 1966, described his first book as follows:

"In his first book — *The Natural World as a Philosophical Problem* (1936) — he turned his attention primarily to the question of the meaning of philosophy, its relationship to the sciences and its role in human life in general. He sees it in an endeavour to create a unified, consistent world-view and to determine man's position within it."

It is clear to me, having known Professor Patočka personally, and as a result of his principled attitude when he signed the Charter and agreed to become one of its first three spokesmen (indeed, the very way he died), that he

The grave of Professor Jan Patočka, one of the first three Charter spokesmen.

had certainly found his own place in the world.

An equally fitting beginning to this chapter might be provided by the unofficial university that bears his name—the Jan Patočka University.

This university does not boast a splendid complex of fine buildings and a student campus. In this respect, too, Czechoslovakia has turned the clock back many centuries, to the time of the universities of Ancient Greece, when the teacher simply gathered his pupils around him, sat down with them in the shade of an olive tree, and began his lecture. The only difference being that in Prague these days there is neither a suitable environment for such activity, nor an olive grove to provide the shade. Young men and women who have been expelled from the country's

Lectures of the unofficial Jan Patočka university.

universities (or who never managed to enrol because of their parents' or their own political views) congregate in private apartments to listen to lectures given by professors and lecturers who have likewise been sacked from the official seats of learning.

Thus Radim Palouš gave talks on the phenomenology of the senses, while Julius Tomin lectured on Aristotle. Foreign experts would visit these unofficial courses, such as Dr I. W. Newton-Smith of Balliol College, Oxford, who lectured on "The Rationale of Science".

And this is where the rationale of power takes a hand in the proceedings.

The lecture is well in progress when the security police raid the flat, manhandle all those present, that very night expel the British philosopher (or Norwegian economist) from the country, and cart the young listeners off to prison, no doubt to show them *their* position in the universal scheme of things. This attempt to educate them according to the lights of the Communist regime is then repeated on a regular basis. The police philosophy behind the operation was succinctly explained to Dr Tomin by one of his interrogators: "So, Mr Tomin, you want the young people what attend your lectures to be able to study, do you? Well, if we let them, they'll start demanding jobs in keeping with their

qualifications. But we also need some people to *work*, Mr Tomin!"

Karl Marx — were he alive today — would probably blush under his voluminous beard. He would undoubtedly be surprised.

Jan Patočka — were *he* alive — would just smile wistfully, for he wouldn't be surprised in the least.

Professor Jan Patočka died at the beginning of March 1977, following a series of interrogations, the last of which lasted a full 12 hours. The secret police outdid themselves during his funeral in the small Prague cemetery of St Margaret's. Early that morning they detained a number of people whom they suspected of intending to attend the funeral. Hundreds of others made their way to the cemetery through a cordon of police patrols, cameramen and photographers who painstakingly took pictures of all those present. Members of Czechoslovakia's motorcycle racing teams raced the engines of their bikes behind the cemetery wall in order to drown out the words of the priest conducting the funeral service, while a police helicopter circled low overhead. Arrests were made. Floral tributes and private rolls of film were confiscated.

This perfected a new method of internment in Bohemia, a method that had first been introduced several years previously during the funeral of Josef Smrkovský and which was to reach its culmination in 1979 with the funeral of Dr František Kriegel, which was not allowed to take place at all.

It is, after all, logical that if "real socialism" and its police forces, secret and uniformed, consider a dead man to be dangerous enough to warrant turning his funeral into police manoeuvres, they must organise even greater police orgies in the case of the living.

A man with two shadows.

That was the headline in a British newspaper which printed these photographs showing Dr František Kriegel, a member of the 1968 Central

Professor Patočka's funeral.

29

Committee of the Czechoslovak Communist Party and now a leading Prague dissident, on one of his walks in the spring of 1977.

It wasn't a very accurate headline, at that, for Dr Kriegel had many more shadows — secret police agents who for several months followed him wherever he went. Only František Kriegel was on his own, and he was exposed to threats and intimidation, endless interrogations and a variety of stunts for which the Czechoslovak political police has a special department.

A small example of what the StB department of

Secret police agents following Dr František Kriegel.

dirty tricks gets up to. A threatening anonymous letter, ingeniously cut not out of a Czech but a French newspaper, signed by the "Free Arab Palestine" group, and containing a message in broken Czech, which might read in English something like this: "Last Warning Against Further Zionist and Spying Activity for Israel".

A black saloon car was parked outside the house where Dr Kriegel lived, at Na Smetance 16, Prague 2, day and night. And the uniformed branch made themselves comfortable on the fourth floor, right in front of Dr Kriegel's apartment, by bringing in a green bench from a nearby park.

The bench was still there months after Dr Kriegel died.

Taking turns in twos, the policemen stopped everyone who dared to visit František Kriegel, demanded identification, carefully noting his or her name and address and reporting it to their higher-ups by radio so that they could decide whether the visitor was to be admitted or not. (Dr Kriegel was not singled out for this kind of treatment. Statement No. 10 by Charter 77, issued in April 1977, stated: "A conservative estimate of the expenses incurred by the authorities over the past two months in the conduct of this surveillance is 350,000 crowns in wages alone." Nobody has estimated the cost during all the years since the beginning of Charter 77.)

The uniformed policemen were busy round the clock, for Dr Kriegel had lots of friends. And many people did not allow themselves to be frightened off and kept coming to see him despite all the harassment.

Luckily for his guardians, he took frequent walks and also visited his friends in his turn. It was

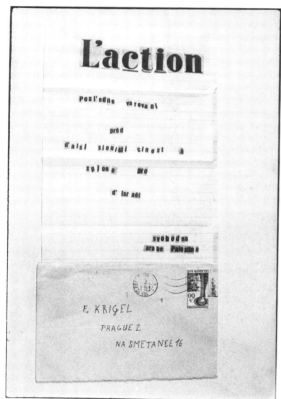

Anonymous letter sent to Dr Kriegel.

during those times that the policemen outside his front door could relax on their park bench, light a cigarette and tip the ash into the empty beer glass from a nearby restaurant. For it was then that responsibility for Dr Kriegel's whereabouts was taken over by the secret police.

Although none of us guessed it at the time, when these pictures were taken Dr František Kriegel had less than a year to live.

Ivan Kyncl took the last snapshot of Dr Kriegel under very strange circumstances.

The only way to describe it is to say that the impossible happened. Just as the writer Bohumil Hrabal put it in his own brilliant way: "In our country even the impossible is possible."

In the summer of 1979 the funeral took place in the crematorium at Prague-Strašnice of Václav Havel's father. Anyone passing the crematorium could tell that this was no ordinary funeral

The deserted police venue in front of Dr Kriegel's flat several months after his death.

because of the police car standing immediately in front of the main entrance. And the several dozen inconspicuous unmarked cars all around, as well as all the "inconspicuous" plain clothes men.

At this time, the playwright and Charter spokesman Václav Havel was spending his third month in a prison cell at Ruzyně, waiting for the trial of VONS members and no one expected him to be allowed to attend his father's funeral. That is because in Czechoslovakia a political prisoner is considered much more dangerous than common criminals such as robbers and murderers. There was no precedent for such a humane act as allowing a "political" to pay his last respects to his father.

Yet they did allow Havel to do so.

Hard to tell why. Whatever their motive, the authorities in this instance did give permission. They might just as easily have made the opposite decision. Aristotle's logic doesn't apply in Czechoslovakia today, only absurdity rules, and its logic is quite different. Its citizens have learned

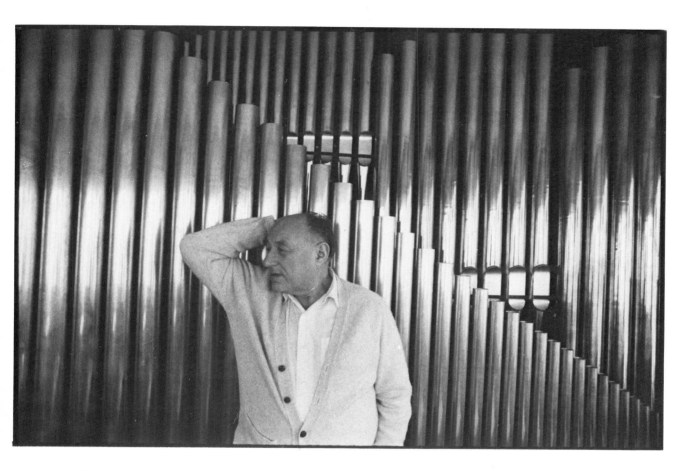

Dr František Kriegel.

to accept any given situation and react to it immediately, without trying to fathom why things have turned out as they have and not another way — knowing full well it is useless.

Shortly before the funeral ceremony a civilian car brought Václav Havel, in civilian clothes, to the crematorium, his escort — also in civvies — accompanying him into the room reserved for the next-of-kin before melting into the crowd of mourners. They evidently had been given orders to stay as inconspicuous as possible, while remaining alert and watchful. With some exaggeration it is possible to say that they succeeded in the first, but they certainly fell down on the rest of their instructions.

As soon as the coffin vanished from sight and the funeral music stopped, the secret policemen were doubtless to have seized Václav Havel and driven him back to his cell at Ruzyně Prison. But they hesitated, and that hesitation was to cost them dear.

*Police car and StB men outside the Prague Crema-
torium during the funeral of playwright Václav
Havel's father.*

The mourners were quicker off the mark,
immediately forming a queue to express their
condolences. Perhaps because there were foreign
journalists present, or perhaps because the
Ministry of the Interior was just then about to
offer Havel his freedom if he accepted an
invitation from a Broadway producer and left for
New York, perhaps simply because the officer in
charge of Havel's escort lost his head ...
whatever the reason, the escort failed to act so
that Václav Havel, who had been cut off from the
outside world for three months, was suddenly
able to learn from his friends what was happening
in that bigger prison cell that is Czechoslovakia.

Watching that funeral ceremony was an eerie
experience. What went through Václav Havel's
mind as he sat in the crematorium? In which of his

Václav Havel and his brother Ivan with their wives at his father's funeral.

future plays will we see a scene based on this morbid, absurd, dramatic situation which even a brilliant, inventive dramatist like Havel would be hard put to dream up.

As he was about to leave the crematorium, Ivan Kyncl was stopped by the police, who demanded that he open up his camera and hand over the exposed film. (This comment, by the way, belongs equally to every picture in this book that was taken in public. And to several that are not in it because the police succeeded in confiscating them.)

Fortunately, the film the policemen outside the crematorium took away with them was a new one, and thus Ivan's pictures of the ceremony and the condolences made it to the pages of western newspapers and now to this book.

The picture of Dr František Kriegel offering his condolences to Václav Havel and giving him the latest news is, most probably, the last ever taken of him. This man, who was the only one of the Czechoslovak politicians who refused to sign the so-called Moscow Agreement after they had been kidnapped by the Russians following the August 1968 invasion, fell ill a mere month after the funeral and died four months later. In his case the police saw to it that there was no funeral ceremony.

But life goes on.

And life, where the Charter 77 people are concerned, is more than funerals, more than police surveillance, interrogation, prison, and all the harassment they have to contend with at the hands of diverse authorities — from the Ministry of the Interior and the police to the departments in charge of traffic, from National Committees to their local street committees. Life would be truly unbearable if all they thought about was that they are not allowed to do the work they had all their

Václav Havel receives condolences and snippets of information at his father's funeral.

37

life considered their vocation, that they were not entitled to a telephone or a driving licence, that the police might break into their homes at any time of the day or night to search it and arrest them, that those of their friends who had not signed the Charter might suddenly begin to avoid them or, on the contrary, start showing a sudden, suspicious interest in all their doings. If they allowed themselves to be destroyed by all this, then the system would have achieved its aim and won a victory.

If a nonconformist is to survive in Czecho-slovakia, he or she must, first of all, learn how to distance himself from all this unpleasantness, learn to lead as normal a life as possible in the midst of abnormality.

However difficult this may be, the Charter people do carry on with their lives.

One of the pieces of information received by Václav Havel at his father's funeral was that VONS — the Committee to Defend the Unjustly Prosecuted — had not stopped working after the arrest of ten of its members. It had acquired new members, mostly young people, it

Václav Havel with Dr František Kriegel.

Dne 3. prosince 1979 nám zemřel ve věku 71 let

MUDr. František Kriegel

Bude zpopelněn v Praze · Motole bez obřadu.

Praha 2, Na Smetance 16

Riva Krieglová
a přátelé

Vytiskly Středočeské tiskárny, n. p. provoz 07, Praha 1, Lípová 6

The announcement of Dr Kriegel's death.

held meetings and issued statements . . .

He was also told that Charter 77 was carrying on its activity, that new signatories had joined it, that the Charter spokesmen continued to meet and work . . .

The people of Charter 77 carried on with their lives. Not just as "dissidents" but as normal human beings. Insofar as this was possible.

They met to celebrate birthdays, as for example that of Dr Gertruda Sekaninová-Čakrtová, a former Czechoslovak diplomat and member of parliament — one of the four MPs who, in October 1968, had the courage to vote against the "temporary" stationing of Soviet troops in Czechoslovakia.

Or Eva Kantůrková, writer and author of screenplays, one of the 500 Czechoslovak writers who are no longer allowed to publish their work.

Yes, some Charter people even got married.

For instance Dr Josef Danisz, whose wedding took place shortly before he was due to start his prison sentence.

Dr Danisz is a young lawyer who defended Charter signatories in court — and did so too well for the regime's liking. He was rewarded by being sacked from his job and sentenced to several months in jail.

(In his case the story has a happy end. Before Dr Danisz was able to start serving his sentence, an amnesty was declared on the occasion of some national holiday or other. In Czechoslovakia nowadays amnesties are carefully arranged in such a way as to affect only thieves, prostitutes and minor criminals, leaving the political prisoners behind bars. By some official oversight, Dr Danisz found himself among those who were amnestied. His case has gone down in Charter history as *lex Danisz*.)

Wedding picture of Dr and Mrs Danisz.

A meeting of the Charter 77 spokesmen.

Former Czechoslovak Member of Parliament and Deputy Foreign Minister, Dr Gertruda Sekaninová-Čakrtová.

Dr Julius Tomin, philosopher, is working on household chores, when he isn't writing protest letters as the one prompted by the brutal assault on his wife (a Charter spokeswoman) who was attacked in the street and had to be hospitalised; when he isn't lecturing at the "Jan Patočka University"; or when he isn't being interrogated at secret police HQ in Bartolomějská Street or examined at the mental clinic (for this Soviet method of dealing with "dissidents" has now come into use in Czechoslovakia).

And if we accept that a philosopher can, in these abnormal circumstances, be spending his time at home cooking dinner, why be surprised that a sociologist (Dr Rudolf Battěk) should be working as a window cleaner? He is by no means the only professional man cleaning Prague shop windows.

Anyone who wants to know more about the life, education and qualifications of a large number of Czechoslovak taxi drivers, stokers, hospital orderlies, warehousemen and unskilled labourers, animal pelt buyers and window cleaners will find the life story of Dr Rudolf Battěk useful as a typical example.

Celebrating the birthday of writer Eva Kanturková.

Born in 1924, studied sociology after the Second World War but was not able to work in his profession until the end of the sixties, during the so-called "liberalisation" period, when he found employment with the Sociological Institute of the Czechoslovak Academy of Sciences. In 1968 he was elected to the Czech National Council, and in 1969 he joined a number of others in signing an open, critical letter to the Prague government. This led to his losing both his job and his position as Member of Parliament, and then to his first arrest; released from prison after a year, he worked as a night watchman, only to be arrested again in 1971 and sentenced to three and a half years' imprisonment on charges of "subversion"; returning from prison with his health impaired, he could not for a long time find any employment, then at last was allowed to work as a window cleaner, but the State Security continued to take an interest in him, repeatedly hauling him in for interrogation and arresting him

Sociologist Ing. Rudolf Battěk.

Philosopher Dr Julius Tomin.

for a day or two at a time; in 1977 he signed Charter 77 and a year later became one of its spokesmen; in 1980 he was fired from his job, again arrested for "subversion", and sentenced to five and a half years in prison. He was still there on his 60th birthday and in early 1985.

A truly typical life story of a Czechoslovak intellectual who refuses to use his head solely as a repository for his hat.

Once, when he was at liberty between two interrogations, we talked to Dr Battěk about a common misunderstanding, which is also typical of Czechoslovak intellectuals. They tend to consider their police interrogators as some kind of "partners" in debate, and in the course of such debates frequently let slip information that is of interest to the secret police.

"I simply cannot rid myself of this bad habit which makes me see the human being behind every policeman," I said to Rudolf Battěk.

"You're absolutely right," he replied. "Instead of grasping the fact that here in Czechoslovakia it would unfortunately make more sense to see the policeman behind every human being."

Witty though his reply was, this is scarcely possible in practice. When the authorities — probably by some administrative oversight and after I had spent a very long time in a vain search for employment — allowed me to earn my living for three months by selling ice-cream at a Prague railway station, I was much more concerned to see, behind every passer-by, a potential customer, little caring at that particular moment what his or her views were as a citizen.

And here is another "typical" case: Zina Freundová, a fourth-year student of Persian and philosophy at Prague's famous Charles University, is working as a waitress. Not, as you might think and as is customary everywhere in the world, in order to help work her way through university: Zina signed the Charter and that was the end of her studies.

How could the Czechoslovak regime of "real socialism" allow people who take seriously the

Student Zina Freundová.

Journalist Karel Kyncl.

documents signed in Helsinki in 1975 to study Persian?

The signatories of Charter 77 — many of them young, as well as artists not allowed to publish, sing, act or exhibit their work and journalists who are forbidden to work in their profession — meet every Thursday afternoon in the Slavia coffee-

43

house, directly opposite the Prague National Theatre.

The regime is trying to force them into isolation by interrogating and "warning" every plumber who comes to their apartment to mend a leaking tap, every friend who, though he himself may not have signed the Charter, is foolish enough to think that he has the right to maintain friendly contacts with whom he pleases.

— so long as you are sensible. Mr Y is an artist, and we have a lot of respect for him, but you must admit that politically speaking he is naïve. On top of which, he's too stubborn to admit it, even to himself. We have to help him — and so have you. Tell us something about his views today, what does he say about Afghanistan, for instance?"

"We know quite a lot about you, wouldn't you say? For instance . . . what is your relationship with

Meeting in the Café Slavia, under police surveillance.

The StB interrogators soon disabuse them of this error:

"Remember that you've got children. Don't you want them to go to university?"

"You hold a responsible position, don't you forget it. But of course you can go on seeing Mr X, after all, he's an old friend of yours. But in your own interest, you should think about your position . . . What did you talk about last time you saw him?"

"I understand you want to go on holiday to Yugoslavia. And why not, there's nothing like a seaside holiday . . . We shan't have any objections

Miss Z? She's a friend, is she? And that's all? Really? . . . Well, in the end, that's your affair. And to some extent also your wife's, eh? Now, don't get on your high horse, we're not here to preach morality. All we're concerned about is the security of the state. And you. Why don't we meet, say once a week or once a fortnight, for a coffee or a glass of brandy and have a little chat. We are very interested in some of your friends . . ."

"On such and such a day in such and such a place you had this to say about our President, Comrade Husák . . . Do you realise that this could get you as much as two years behind bars? Oh yes, according

to paragraph 103 . . . But we'll forget all about your little indiscretion if you . . ."

"Now, you're a Party member . . . how do you think your friendship with Mr A chimes with your Party membership? Do we have to tell you what is your duty as a comrade?"

Perhaps it is just because the regime is doing its damndest to confine them in a ghetto, surrounded by an impermeable wall of spies and informers, that those people in Prague at least try to pretend they are leading a normal life. Perhaps that is the reason they meet every Thursday afternoon in the Slavia coffee-house, regularly and openly, drinking their cup of coffee, their carafe of wine or glass of brandy, doing what intellectuals do the world over: They talk and discuss various topics.

Nearby tables are occupied by inconspicuous-looking gentlemen with briefcases or by girls

equipped with prominent busts and microphones, by photographers whose pictures appear only in the archives of the secret police.

And that is how the following sentence then appears in an indictment, as was the case with the members of the Committee to Defend the Unjustly Prosecuted: "The group held conspiratorial meetings, first in the Slavia coffee-house and later in private homes" . . .

The last two photos from the Slavia coffee-house accurately capture the atmosphere of the Prague Winter.

In the first, a Charter spokesman, Dr Ladislav Lis, is pointing to the seemingly innocent young man behind him, who is nonchalantly sipping water from his glass. He is one of the team of StB agents whose duty that day was to maintain surveillance on Dr Lis. The other picture shows the same young man at his strategically and tactically convenient post, sitting alone at his table. One of the many employees of Big Brother, who keeps watching.

Historian Dr Jan Tesař: his first hour of "freedom" after five years in jail.

But time marches on and life continues.

Now and again someone returns from jail — after a few days, a few months, or also a few years.

The historian, Dr Jan Tesař, after five years in prison.

The journalist, Jiří Lederer, after three years in prison.

And someone else goes to jail.

Like the young graphic artist, Pavel Büchler.

Now and again someone decides to sever the

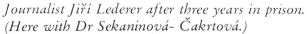

Journalist Jiří Lederer after three years in prison.
(Here with Dr Sekaninová- Čakrtová.)

Pavel Büchler's trial.

links binding him or her to Czechoslovakia, to the cobbles of Old Town Square, the queues outside the shops and, above all, to friends and relatives. They apply for permission to emigrate, undergo an incredibly complicated Calvary, getting together all the necessary documents, certificates, recommendations and approvals, answering questions during police interrogations, compulsorily renouncing all claims to a pension,

paying a high ransom for themselves and every member of their family — and then they will leave the country.

Before they do so, friends will come and say goodbye, taking a last look round the now empty apartment — in this particular case that of the former TV journalist, Vladimir Škutina.

At Prague's main railway station, friends say

Designer Pavel Büchler being taken to court under escort.

In an empty flat of journalist Vladimír Škutina following his departure for abroad.

Saying goodbye to journalist Oldřich Unger and his family as they leave Prague to emigrate.

goodbye to the former radio journalist, Oldřich Unger — who never took part in anything political, his speciality on Prague Radio being ornithology and especially birds' voices — his wife and three sons.

Saying goodbye at the Airport in Ruzyně — just a little distance from the most "famous" Prague prison, in whose cells he had spent many months — was the already mentioned historian, Dr Jan Tesař.

Another one to leave Czechoslovakia is the painter and illustrator, Karel Havlíček, his wife

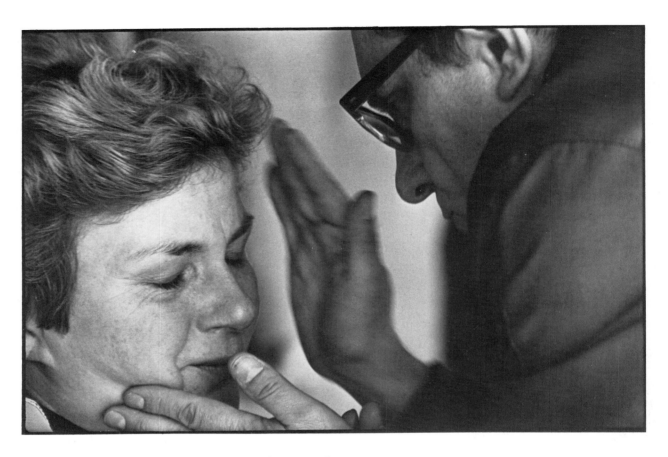

Historian Dr Jan Tesař about to emigrate.

and small son.

But since they left from Bratislava, we don't have any pictures of their farewell. What we do have is a series of photos taken at the private view of Karel Havlíček's last exhibition in his own country, which took place in the small provincial town of Sázava. It was a public exhibition in a way — but in a way it wasn't. Many Charter signatories took part, ably assisted by the police and police cars on every road leading to the town.

The "exhibition hall" was the dining-room of writer Pavel Kohout's house in Sázava.

Author Pavel Kohout (left) opening the unofficial exhibition of drawings by artist Karel Havlíček in Kohout's dining-room.

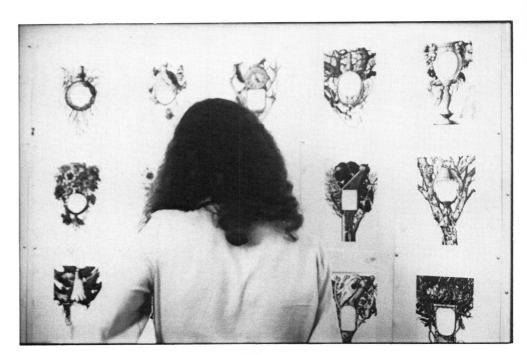

Private view of Karel Havlíček's exhibition.

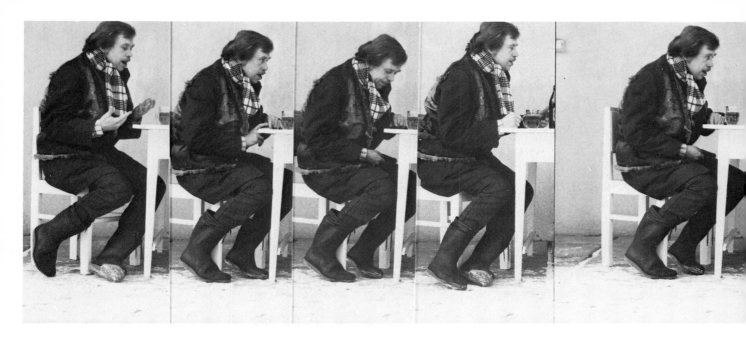

Václav Havel and Pavel Landovský.

When they attended the opening of Havlíček's exhibition, the playwright Václav Havel and actor Pavel Landovský brought with them a stereo recording of Havel's play, *Audience.*

It was a professional job.

The Cast: Maltster ...... Pavel Landovský

Ferdinand .... Václav Havel

Director:?

Technician:?

The tape has since been copied many times and is circulating all over the country, copies being made of copies, until some of them are barely audible.

A year later the play came out abroad in the form of a gramophone record, with a cover by Karel Havlíček and Ivan Kyncl.

It is in the arts that we get what is perhaps the most horrifying picture of Czechoslovakia's "real socialism". It is reflected there literally — as for instance in Havel's plays and the novels, stories and essays of several dozen other writers — but also figuratively speaking.

How else to describe a situation, in which hundreds of artists in every sphere of the arts (from literature to the plastic arts, the theatre and music) are prevented from taking any part in creative work.

The authorities have issued a list of some five hundred writers whose books had to be removed from all public libraries and who are not to be published by any Czechoslovak publishing house, performed in any theatre, in the cinema or on television or radio. The result can be judged simply by comparing the quality of contemporary

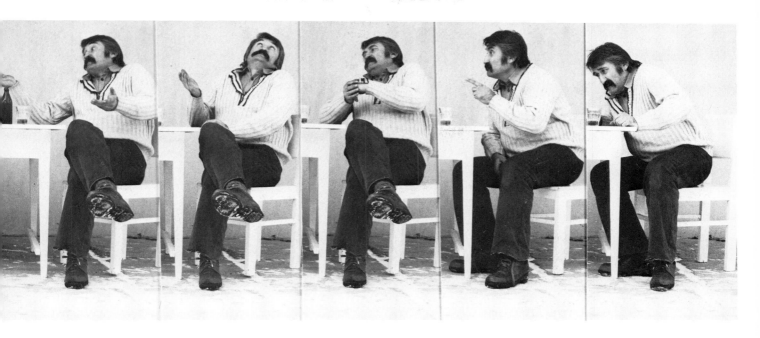

official Czechoslovak literary output with the volumes that appear in "Petlice" (Padlock), "Expedice" (Dispatch), "Kvart" (Quarto) and the other samizdat series.

Such a comparison will show quite clearly that the powers-that-be have excluded the best authors from Czechoslovak literature.

Excluded?

Maybe that is not the right word. Rather, they have been driven underground. Their books, laboriously retyped, circulate in a small number of copies, many of them badly legible and reaching only a few hundred readers, but it is these books which will prove to be the ones that will stand the test of time.

Samizdat, however, is not the only way banned authors can get published. The abnormal condi-

Sleeve of gramophone record (made in Sweden) with the Czech recording of Audience *by Václav Havel.*

Some of the banned books by Czechoslovak writers which have come out in samizdat.

tions of life in Czechoslovakia since 1968 have given rise to a strange profession which Czech slang calls "cover men" (or, in English, front men). Those who are allowed to publish lend their names to those who are not. And so in Czechoslovakia today writers who have been blacklisted by the regime — both original authors and translators — manage to get their books printed, their plays performed, their screenplays filmed, their stories or articles published in obscure newspapers. None of these are exactly masterpieces, for the official cultural policy favours mediocrity and anything that might show signs of excellence would be suspect. But the authors benefit in a number of ways.

1. They earn at least a minimal wage.
2. They get a certain amount of creative satisfaction from being able to pick up a book they have written, see a play they have authored, see their story or poem in print and
3. They gain an insight into the human psyche, as there are various types of front men. Some are highly courageous and selfless, whom you would mortally offend were you to offer them a pecuniary reward, while others are cold-blooded businessmen who will demand as much as a third or even half of your fee for the honour of having your work come out under their name.

This aspect of life in present-day Czechoslovakia will provide future historians with a great deal of research material. It would lend itself to a whole series of newspaper articles, complete with photographs, if only . . . if only we were not dealing with today's Czechoslovakia, where even the slightest factual reference to the people concerned would endanger their jobs and even their personal liberty.

Every writer produces his work for his readers, listeners and viewers. If the authorities deprive him of his audience, they on the one hand free him from the demands of censorship and self-censorship, but on the other they make him suffer stressful traumas resulting from his awareness that his life is being wasted and his talent and professional skill made to lie fallow. Not everyone has the strength of character to be able to write "for the drawer" in the knowledge that he may never be read. It is quite possible to be an optimist *sub specie aeternitatis*, but no individual lives forever. We shall never know how much irreparable damage Czechoslovakia's "real socialism" has caused also in this respect.

The aforementioned meetings in the Slavia

coffee-house are one kind of attempt to break out of the enforced isolation.

The community of Charter 77 undoubtedly represents another such attempt.

As does the "Padlock" samizdat series, and other such editions.

And the "Jan Patočka University".

And the various scientific and artistic seminars.

And the performances by various solo musicians or groups in private apartments, in country barns and in the open air.

And the "Living Room Theatre" of Vlasta Chramostová.

Vlasta Chramostová is no ordinary actress. It would be no exaggeration to describe her as a

Actress Vlasta Chramostová and her husband, film cameraman Stanislav Milota.

A performance of the Living Room Theatre.

symbol, as the personification of the resistance of a cultured human being to totalitarian stupidity and the dehumanised obtuseness of power.

She is one of Czechoslovakia's best theatre and film actresses; even the regime, attempting to classify almost everything, many years ago awarded her the title of "meritorious artist". But in August 1968, during the Soviet-led invasion of Czechoslovakia, she played in real life a role which that same regime regarded as unforgivable: the role of assistant to her husband, Stanislav Milota, an outstanding Czech cameraman who, in the streets of Prague, documented the end of "socialism with a human face" and the beginning of "armoured socialism". And she had the gall not to "recant", to remain loyal to her friends at a time when that meant the certain end of her career.

The logic of the powers-that-be in such cases tends to be very logical indeed: *You are not with us, therefore you're against us, and therefore you must be destroyed. You must be eradicated from the people's minds and memory. If you're an actress, you may not act. If you're a cameraman, you may not shoot films.*

It has to be understood that hardly anyone has actually been notified that they are forbidden to lecture at a university, to work as a scientist, a historian, a journalist, sociologist, philosopher, actor. That would be dangerous, for those who issue such orders might one day be called to account — but it is also unnecessary. All that is needed is not to renew a contract, or to terminate someone's employment on the grounds of "reorganisation".

Such a person will then not find a job in his or her profession, for to be given one he has first to undergo a "personnel screening" process. This includes information provided by the Party and trades union organisation in his former place of employment as well as from his neighbourhood committees, which guarantee continuity of information about every citizen from the cradle to the grave. The citizen himself is also required to express his political and other views, having to complete a long questionnaire every time he applies for a job, which will pose questions such as: *What was your attitude in the year 1968 and how do you view the fraternal international assistance given to Czechoslovakia by the countries of the Warsaw Pact in August 1968?*

There is only one possible reply to that question if the applicant wishes to stay in his profession, if the scientist or technician wishes to have access to scientific libraries and laboratories, if a writer wishes to continue writing and publishing, if an actor wishes to act and a singer sing. First and foremost, he or she must carry out what is known as "self-criticism":

Admit that prior to the Soviet invasion — and possibly even for some time afterwards — he allowed himself to be misled by the "counter-revolutionaries". (It is advisable to name names here, or at the very least to put the blame on the counter-revolutionary activities of the mass media at the time.)

Recognise the Soviet invasion and occupation as fraternal assistance.

Pledge to take an active part in the building of real socialism, whatever that may mean.

Those who played a part in Czechoslovakia's public life were — and are — required to make these statements in public.

Yet even the man or woman who decides to do so and thus besmirch him- or herself cannot be certain of making it. It is then up to the Party and police authorities whether they will accept the recantation.

If they do, he or she can carry on working in their own profession, doing their utmost to bury the memory of their shame deep in their subconscious.

If not, the shame is all they are left with.

Black lists? A capitalist survival, comrades. True, at one time these ancient black lists did provide us with an effective weapon against those who refused to accommodate themselves to the changed conditions, but socialism has since then undergone many revolutionary changes and has discarded them on the rubbish-heap of history. Today, we have other, far more effective, indeed totally effective, means to deal with people who refuse to go along with us. They can do what they like, they cannot escape reality. When they're looking for a job, they can't go to individual capitalists who might possibly display dangerous liberal tendencies and lend a sinner a helping hand. Today, everyone, whatever job they seek, has to apply to society. And society, that is us! Power! Total power! If we wish, we can condemn anyone in this country to death by starvation.

What's that? You think I'm exaggerating? That everybody has a certain number of friends who might be willing to provide financial assistance or even feed him and his family? Don't be ridiculous! Anyone we decide merits death by starvation is a criminal. A person who has committed the criminal act of dissent! And for that we have paragraph 165 in our Criminal Code: 'Approving a criminal act.'

And that is just the most primitive of the many weapons we have at our disposal . . .

But to return to Vlasta Chramostová.

After 1969, there suddenly was no work for her in any Czech theatre, nor in films, on radio and television. The regime allowed her to stay in this limbo for a few months, to bring home to her the realisation that she could only hope to work if she fell into line. And then they proffered a helping finger, allowing her to appear on the stage of a provincial theatre a long way from Prague. Her title role in Bertolt Brecht's *Mother Courage* raised that small theatre to unforeseen prominence as people drove hundreds of kilometres to see her. To see Chramostová act. To see Courage on the stage.

The authorities quickly realised their mistake. Vlasta Chramostová was quite obviously not grateful for the opportunity they had given her, she simply refused to go down on her knees and beg their forgiveness.

More severe punishment was thus required: she was no longer to be allowed to act even in the provinces.

In the years that followed, Vlasta Chramostová used her talent to manufacture shades for table lamps. They were attractive shades for attractive table-lamps — but for a born actress it was impossible to replace footlights with table-lamps forever.

In 1976, the greatest Czech living poet, Jaroslav Seifert celebrated his 75th birthday. Chramostová arranged a private reading for him and his friends from Seifert's own memoirs, *All the Beauties of the World*, then still only in manuscript. A banned actress reading the work of a banned poet.

Later, in her own apartment just above the Prague National Museum, she repeated the Seifert reading for small groups of friends and poetry lovers. They came, sometimes fifteen, sometimes twenty-five of them, occupied the available chairs and settees or sat on the floor, and listened.

The "Living Room Theatre" was born.

Vlasta Chramostová and Jaroslav Seifert.

Shakespeare's Macbeth *in the Living Room Theatre of Vlasta Chramostová.*

Jaroslav Seifert, winner of the 1984 Nobel Prize for Literature, became the first author played by this unique theatre. *All the Beauties of the World* is not a political work; the most convincing proof is that when the regime finally realised the possible "danger" of Seifert being awarded the Nobel Prize it hastily published the book with only a few passages censored — to demonstrate to the outside world that the poet was not banned after all. But in 1976-79 the Czechoslovak secret police regarded readings from his book in private flats as "unauthorised meetings" and "anti-socialist activities".

Seifert, who was one of the original signatories

of Charter 77, earned the long-lasting hatred of the regime both by his poetry and his views and the way he expressed them. Not his political views in the true sense of the word, though on the other hand in a totalitarian system *everything* is treated as political; the most dangerous people are those who display sincerity, decency, tolerance, and who stick up for their principles. When Vlasta Chramostová, in her Living Room Theatre, began to read excerpts from Seifert's latest work, the poet had again been more than six years on the *index librorum prohibitorum*. It is an indirect yet highly significant proof of his greatness that even then he could only be silenced selectively: some of his earlier poetry did keep appearing from time to time in various collections, for it was impossible to remove him entirely from Czech literature. His readers refused to forget him. And when, in 1979, the secret police intercepted a letter addressed to the Swedish Academy in which a number of silenced Czech writers proposed Seifert for the Nobel Prize, the regime got cold feet, anticipating an international scandal should Jaroslav Seifert really obtain the award. And so, just 10 years late, in 1980 the more recent of Seifert's works started coming out in the state houses.

It can be said that Jaroslav Seifert survived his own death by the strength of his poetry. But poetry can only survive thanks to people who read it, appreciate it and love it. In this sense Vlasta Chramostová truly reflected the genuine feelings of the vast majority of her fellow countrymen.

By the end of 1979 the "Living Room Theatre" put on its fourth première.

Let us, however, say a few words about the third première. This was a performance of Shakespeare's *Macbeth*, produced by the banned playwright Pavel Kohout.

The 25 characters and numerous extras in this Shakespeare play, for whom even the stage of a large theatre tends to be small, were played by five people on less than 30 square metres of a living-room floor. There were two professional actors — Vlasta Chramostová and Pavel Landovský — and three non-actors — singer and writer Vlastimil Třešňák, writer Pavel Kohout, and his daughter Tereza, at that time forced to earn her living as a charwoman.

The State Security tolerated only 17 performances before coming to the irrevocable conclusion that William Shakespeare (1564-1616) was an enemy of real socialism and had to be silenced.

As is their habit, they tried harassment first. One evening, shortly before the play was due to end, 15 uniformed policemen turned up at Vlasta Chramostová's flat. They told her that they had received reports of an orgy taking place there and that they intended to identify all those present.

While her husband, Stanislav Milota, argued with the policemen out in the hall, and while Macbeth (Pavel Landovský) was about to be killed by Macduff (Pavel Kohout), in front of an

63

Police cars outside the house where the Living Room Theatre is performing Macbeth.

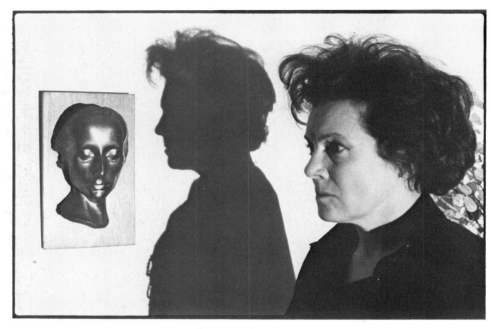

Vlasta Chramostová in front of the death mask of 19th century/writer Božena Němcová.

Playwright František Pavlíček.

audience of some 20 people in the living room, Ivan Kyncl leaned out of the window to take a documentary picture of some distinctly non-Shakespearean police cars down below in a dark Prague street.

Meanwhile, on the stage of the "Living Room Theatre", a royal criminal and tyrant had met his death to the sound of the last words of this famous tragedy about the triumph of right and justice:

> *... What's more to do,*
> *Which could be planted newly with the time,*
> *As calling home our exiled friends abroad*
> *That fled the snares of watchful tyranny,*
> *Producing forth the cruel ministers*
> *Of this dead butcher and his fiend-like queen,*
> *Who, as 'tis thought, by self and violent hands*
> *Took off her life; this, and what needful else*
> *That calls upon us by the grace of Grace*
> *We will perform in measure, time and place ...*

65

Pavlíček's play about Božena Němcová in the Living Room Theatre.

The audience did not applaud, for this might have been regarded by the "cruel ministers" as evidence of the "reported" orgies. Or as a disturbance of the peace. Instead, actors and spectators alike got their ID cards ready for inspection.

But even this sort of harassment failed to produce results — the Living Room Theatre gave guest performances in other people's apartments, and so the police were forced to employ heavier artillery against William Shakespeare. They began to block access to houses in which they suspected *Macbeth* was about to be performed. Only people who could prove they lived there would be allowed to enter. No one else — no matter what their reason, or whom they wished to visit.

And so at last the StB won a famous victory over William Shakespeare.

In December 1979, another première — the fourth — took place in the Living Room Theatre.

In front of the death mask of the tragic Czech writer of the 19th century, Božena Němcová (no stage prop this, for it adorned Vlasta Chramostová's wall long before the Living Room Theatre came into being) the actress performs the story of the author's life.

The first Czech monodrama — a form of one man (or woman) show born of necessity. The five characters were all portrayed by the banned actress, Vlasta Chramostová. Author: banned playwright, František Pavlíček.

On Friday, 25 January 1980, as he mounted the dark staircase outside Vlasta Chramostová's apartment, Ivan Kyncl encountered some 15 people who had come to see the show, and among them both uniformed and plainclothed policemen. They were asking to see everyone's ID cards and said no one was allowed inside. Ivan had his photographer's bag and cameras with him. He took out one camera and slung it around his neck.

"I hope you don't think you're going to take photographs here?" said one of the policemen in a sharp tone of voice.

"Of course not," replied Ivan, and pressed the release. The camera was equipped with an automatic reel winder, but as this made a whirring noise, he could not use it, resorting to manual winding instead. And he took another snapshot, and a third.

Needless to say, the lighting was far from perfect, the circumstances somewhat difficult . . .

Thus the photograph, printed here against its author's wishes, is not a good one. You may say we could have achieved the same result by printing a rectangle and filling it with printer's ink. Well, the photographer is of the same opinion.

Nevertheless, I cannot resist feeling that those blurred silhouettes provide a realistic document of the life of members of Charter 77.

The reader should know that this far from perfect photo has twice been in the hands of the Czechoslovak police, survived a search of its author's person, travelled 90 kilometres in a police car to North Bohemia, was carried through the deserted streets of Dolní Bousov an hour after midnight and then hidden from other police vehicles, arriving in Prague only the following morning. All this just to reveal several frames which, when developed, showed these indistinct silhouettes.

A tragedy?

Or a comedy?

A tragicomedy.

I would say that the shadows on the previous page, the darkness, the dichotomy between comedy and tragedy, all give a pretty accurate

picture of present-day Czechoslovak reality.

This is how Ivan himself describes what took place:

Two of us — Charter spokesman Rudolf Battěk and I — were led away from the staircase and detained; naturally, without any reasons being given. We were still descending the stairs when one of the secret policemen took my camera and the

Members of the audience detained by the police outside the flat.

cassette with the exposed film and handed it to a uniformed colleague.

When, a little later, the plainclothed guy was out of earshot I said to the other one: "Listen, that camera is terribly expensive. Why don't you give it to me to carry. You could never pay for it."

He was a young fellow and probably inexperienced. And of course not from the StB. He handed the camera back to me.

I had already wound the exposed film back into the cassette, and all I had to do now was to open the camera unobtrusively and take out the cassette... Only just at that moment the StB man caught up with us. "Hand that camera to the officer at once!"

There was nothing for it. On our way to the police car I at least got a new cassette ready in my pocket, just in case...

The young man holding my camera sat in front next to the driver, while Rudolf Battěk, a uniformed policeman and I sat in the back. There was no room for anyone else, and so we were without any StB men.

"Let me put the cover on the lens," I said to the young policeman when the car started off in the direction of police headquarters in Bartolomějská Street. "I'm worried about that camera, you know — it cost forty thousand crowns."

Incredible as it may seem, he passed it back to me. Was it really only his inexperience? I don't know.

Quickly I opened the camera and withdrew the cassette with the exposed film.

"What do you think you're doing?" yelled the policeman next to Rudolf Battěk, clawing at the camera across him. "Hand over that film!"

"But of course. Just a sec. ..."

I dropped the exposed film on the floor, fished the new cassette out of my pocket and handed it to him, I'd rather not say what I did with the exposed film — why unnecessarily give professional secrets away to the Czechoslovak police? Both Rudolf Battěk and I were searched when we got to Bartolomějská; we had to empty our pockets, and then the policemen frisked us. They did not find the cassette with the pictures I took on the staircase.

They handcuffed us, put each in a different, unmarked car, and drove us through the dark streets of the city and out along the main road to Mladá Boleslav. At about 22.15 we arrived at Dolní Bousov in the Jičín district, where the car stopped outside the local police station. My escort of two uniformed policemen led me upstairs to the first floor. They removed my handcuffs and interrogated me. The usual stuff, questions mixed with threats and eloquent gestures, such as slamming their right fist into the palm of their left hand. After a few minutes one of my interrogators opened the door and I saw two others leading Rudolf Battěk along the corridor. The door was slammed shut.

"Well, how about you," asked one of the policemen, "you also feel like laughing?"

"More like weeping," I said.

At half past twelve that night they took me downstairs and shoved me out into the street. "Scram!"

"Aren't you going to take me back to Prague?" I asked, superfluously.

This made them laugh. "What else can we do for you?"

Outside stood four parked cars — two police vehicles and two civilian ones. I had been brought here in one of these, and I supposed Rudolf Battěk had travelled in the other.

I walked towards the town square, but I had only gone some three hundred metres when I heard a car start behind me. I realised that it was not all over yet. They hadn't even broken my camera, just confiscated the films ... I slipped into the nearest doorway and waited. A police car drove past me and circled the square, as if looking for someone. As if? I followed the rails to the station and asked where I was. The name Dolní Bousov meant nothing to me. A lone railwayman allowed me to phone home, and then I quickly left the station — only just in time, for a minute later the police car appeared on the scene.

It had been my intention to try and catch a lift, since the next train went in four hours, but now I decided to leave this place as quickly as possible.

Illegal concert of two groups of the Czech underground — "Plastic People of the Universe" and "DG 307".

Avoiding the road, I made my way across snow-covered fields to Sobotka, and then by train and bus to Prague. I had plenty of time to think during the long journey, and I told myself I would leave this hospitable country of my own accord, rather than wait for them to throw me out, as they promised to do when interrogating me at Dolní Bousov.

But for the next few months, Ivan still took photographs in Czechoslovakia — mainly of the members and activities of Charter 77.

At night, he locked 75 houses in the Little Quarter, this being the most qualified job he was allowed to do. During the day — and sometimes also at night — he took pictures.

Working morale in Czechoslovakia is so low that it didn't strike anyone as strange that 75 houses in the Little Quarter often remained unlocked all night. At least on those nights when he could be sure that an inconspicuous car with its lights off and its engine running was not parked in one of the small side streets, its three occupants smoking cigarette after cigarette to pass the time.

Some nights Ivan managed to get away for a long trip, accompanying several friends on their way to West Bohemia where, in an isolated barn, the Plastic People of the Universe put on a concert.

Czech underground music.

As far removed from socialist realism as anything can be.

Not that I have any sympathy for socialist realism, but I would be lying if I said I liked the music of the underground. Nevertheless, it does seem perverse that the authorities should officially prohibit the Plastic People from playing and singing — not to mention that they should send them to prison for it.

I confided my views to the author of these photographs, and got told off.

Not because the Plastic People of the Universe would have won him over by that concert (I believe he still prefers Bach or New Orleans jazz), but he was incensed that I dared to criticise music which I had only heard on one or two tapes. And

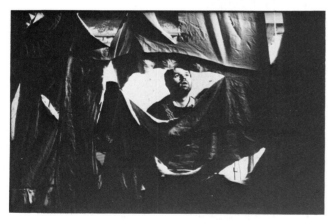

he expounded on the atmosphere of that concert, a dream-like, unreal atmosphere, giving the sense of a small desert island in a hostile ocean which may at any time blow a storm and wipe it off the face of the earth. And he told me how, under such circumstances, one listened with greater feeling and understanding to music which, in the relative peace of his own room, might strike him as strange and incomprehensible.

I expect he is right.

No, I *know* he is right.

It occurred to me how, years ago, I had in much the same way first grown to understand and then admire abstract painters, the theatre of the absurd, and even Franz Kafka. What had helped change my mind about all these was the realisation that Czechoslovak socialist reality was incomparably more absurd than Kafka. That, compared to our everyday lives, Ionesco or Beckett might almost seem like socialist realists.

Similarly I now realised what a remarkable group of people was Charter 77. It had brought together such diverse people, representatives of different and often contrasting philosophies and political opinions. At first sight it might appear that these people were only united by negative things, by their opposition to the thuggish system which ruled the country against its people's will. But I don't think it is as simple and primitive as that. The positive elements which link the signatories of the Charter can, in brief, be expressed as follows:

Historical optimism.

Common sense.

Feelings of responsibility, honour and human dignity.

Tolerance.

The environment in which the Charter exists is anything but idyllic, and I would not like the reader to think that I am trying to portray the Charter itself and conditions within it as some kind of idyll. That would be both absurd and naïve. Nothing in this world is purely black and white, however much we all may at times wish it to be so.

But it is a fact that the "minimal" programme of Charter 77 has been accepted by people of practically every shade of opinion. It is when they come to discuss their ideas concerning a "maximal" programme, their concept of the future and ways of achieving it, that they naturally differ; they make no secret of these differences, and they hold impassioned discussions among themselves. The secret police follows these discussions with unconcealed satisfaction, interpreting them as signs of the Charter's disintegration. (In this, unfortunately, they sometimes come to the same erroneous conclusion as some Western journalists whose knowledge of the situation leaves much more to be desired.)

It can, of course, happen that arguments among the powerless can turn into storms in teacups marked by an excess of chauvinism and hate. Despite the fierce repression and persecution to which its members have been subjected, Charter 77 has not gone down this road and has survived for more than eight years now; and unless the authorities resort to mass arrests (not to mention executions, as was the case in the 1950s), it will certainly continue to exist. Indeed, I doubt whether even the most brutal mass terror could eradicate all the roots which have given rise to the Charter, roots which exist in every human being without exception, being the nuclei of the most basic characteristics which make us human. And even if they lie dormant for years and whole decades, giving the outward appearance that they have perished, it only takes a small change in the individual's environment for these roots to come to life ...

Rudé právo (the main Communist Party daily in Prague) writes day in, day out that "our people unanimously condemns", "agrees", "approves" this, that or the other, that "the inhabitants have once again demonstrated the unity of our Party with the people", "the unity of the socialist camp", and many other unities. Yet every reader of *Rudé právo* knows that these are lies, that it would be far truer to say that the people are united *against* the Communist Party. And I suspect that is known also to the authors of those articles and editorials.

Against this background of a non-existent but constantly proclaimed unity, I find the discussions (and even arguments) within Charter 77 to be a breath of fresh air in a stuffy, smoke-filled room, an embryo of normality in the stomach of an abnormal, inhuman Golem made of clay.

An embryo of normality ...

The expression conjures up an image of something that is just beginning, something new being created, a child being born.

Whenever I had to deal with a particularly nasty, malicious or arrogant StB interrogator or prison warder, I tried to imagine what these gentlemen looked like when they were babies. And I thought they were probably charming, with delightful little creases on their bottoms, prattling away sixteen to the dozen in baby talk ... and now look at them!

All babies are innocent and charming, like hunks of plasticine waiting for life to mould them one way or another.

The children of the Charter signatories — that would in itself be a subject for a book.

As far as the state authorities are concerned, they are born irreparably damaged and crippled, no matter how wealthy, beautiful or intelligent they may be. Their parents are "dissidents", and that can have worse consequences than if the baby was born with a physical or mental handicap. Evil fairies, in the shape of personnel managers, determine their future while they are still in the cradle, permitting them only elementary education and later the least congenial and worse paid job with little prospect of promotion.

Not even the most elitist social system in the world practices this kind of social determinism. Compared to a "dissident's" son or daughter's chances of acquiring university (or even secondary) education, it was child's play for a slave in ancient Rome to become rich, secure his release and join the ranks of the patricians.

Real socialism also pays a great deal of attention to the *emotional* development of "dissident" children.

The security agents who carry out surveillance (or those among them whose task is to intimidate their victims by tailing them as conspicuously as possible) cannot, naturally, waive their responsible duty out of consideration for children, who may be accompanying their father or mother on a walk or a shopping trip, or who may be taken by their parents to a playground. What if this is just a trick, with the child being taken along only to camouflage some counter-revolutionary or subversive activity?

When carrying out a house search, policemen can hardly be expected to miss out the child's cot, an obvious place of concealment for anti-state documents.

And the children will grow to appreciate how skilfully the policemen break down doors, seize their father or mother and drag them away into the unknown.

No less effective are the visits the children pay to their parents in prison, with the screws in attendance, who rejoice in the fine title of "Mr Educator".

Apart from which, there are always neighbours and even teachers who consider these "dissident" children as suitable material to demonstrate their own socialist commitment on.

It should be said in all fairness that there are far fewer such neighbours and teachers than there used to be.

(Used to be? Yes, that's right, this is nothing new in Czechoslovakia. Similar, and even worse, treatment used to be meted out to the children of "class enemies", "kulaks", "capitalist elements", "the faithful", and other outcasts, and sometimes also the children of highly-placed Communist officials who fell victim to Stalin's and Gottwald's purges. Both sons of the Regional

Singer Charlie Soukup with wife and children.

The family of the priest, Tomas Bísek.

Party Secretary Ota Šling, who was one of those tried and executed during the Slánský trial in the 1950s, recall how the director of the children's home to which they were sent ordered them to write an essay on the "Just punishment of the traitors belonging to the anti-state conspiratorial centre led by Rudolf Slánský".)

These days, on the contrary, people — those, at least, who do not belong to the police force — try to behave as well as they can towards the children of "dissidents". That is, normally. And if the

Charter community had achieved nothing else but given these children a large number of "uncles" and "aunts" who love them and let them see they do, it would have done a great deal. Thanks to this, the children, unlike their predecessors in the fifties, have known less fear and helplessness. The obtuseness of the policemen is compensated by much kindness and love, not all of it by any means coming only from their immediate families.

This photo was "commissioned", being intended as a greeting to be sent to prison to Dr

St Nicholas Day presents for the children of Charter signatories jailed in political trials.

The children of Charter 77 spokesman Dr Václav Benda, sentenced to four years' imprisonment.

Václav Benda, the father of the five children in the picture.

The youngest, who is the darling of the family and of all the Prague signatories of Charter 77, is called Philip Benda.

You should see how his eyes light up when one of his two older brothers reads him a further episode of the fairy tale his father sends in his letters from prison. Apart from a dragon and other customary fairy-tale characters, the whole Benda family also appears in it, and little Philip never fails to quote a sentence from an early episode: "Little Philip is a clever lad!"

By the way, talking of little Philip Benda, I can give the Czechoslovak secret police a tip how to knock the breath out of Zdena Tomin, the otherwise very eloquent spokeswoman of the

Charter spokeswoman Zdena Tomin with little Philip Benda.

Charter. I offer it without any claim to remuneration:

Zdena Tomin once inadvertently promised Philip that she would buy him a puppy for his birthday. A toy, understandably, because there are enough living beings in the family already. Since then, whenever she appeared in the doorway, Philip would ask: "Auntie Zdena, have you brought me the puppy?"

"On your birthday, Philip," Zdena Tomin would reply. But she only held out for some two weeks, then she capitulated and brought him the toy.

"Nice Auntie," Philip praised her. "Will you bring a kitten on my birthday?"

Zdena Tomin swallowed hard, resisted for a week or so, and then bought him the kitten.

"It's lovely," enthused little Philip. "Will you give me a monkey for my birthday?"

Three or four days later, the author of the photographs in this book got to know about Philip's request. He bought a tiny monkey on a rubber band and gave it to the boy. "Philip," he interrupted the child's thank yous, "next time Auntie Zdena comes, ask her for an elephant."

And Philip Benda, being truly "a clever lad", made a mental note, so that when Zdena Tomin turned up that evening and, as she took her coat off in the hall rummaged in her bag to find the toy monkey and called out to him: "You know what I've brought you, Philip?"

Little Philip ran towards her, shouting happily: "An elephant!"

When you are together with the Benda children — little Philip and Patrick, Martha, Mark and Martin — you can easily forget the harsh reality outside their apartment in Charles Square, but the illusion never lasts long.

The door will open and someone will come in with news of yet another interrogation, of another friend who has had a police guard placed on his doorstep so that no one is allowed to visit him, or had his house turned upside down during a police search, his telephone or driving licence taken away, car tyres slashed . . .

Or someone opens a window and you look out and see:

From a window in the Bendas' apartment you can see the corner of the building of the Municipal Court where all the Prague political trials are held. Or at least most of them. In October 1979 Dr Václav Benda was on trial there, together with five other members of VONS, the Committee to Defend the Unjustly Prosecuted.

On the next page you can clearly see the camera, installed in the window of the Municipal Court building in May 1979 in order to keep an eye on the vicinity of Dr Benda's apartment, when he was a spokesman of Charter 77 and its meet-

ings took place at his home.

A few weeks later the VONS members were arrested.

The camera remained in place. It was still there in the autumn, when the six VONS members went on trial, and for a whole month afterwards.

Then these pictures appeared in Western newspapers, and the camera was no longer to be seen. No, it was not removed — they simply covered it with a black cloth, so that it became almost invisible at a distance. In the first few days, those responsible did not bring enough cloth to

Building of the Prague Municipal Court, as seen from the window of Václav Benda's flat in which meetings of the Committee to Defend the Unjustly Prosecuted took place.

cover the green tripod on which the camera was mounted, and this remained clearly visible.

"You forgot the tripod!" said Dr Kamila Bendová, out loud to make sure the bugging equipment got the message. "You must cover the camera tripod."

And those responsible for camouflaging the camera did as she suggested.

However, no one bothered to remove or camouflage the cable leading from the camera to a window on the second floor of the court building. That window belongs to the office of the President of the Municipal Court, Dr Kašpar. Inside, the cable is attached to a TV screen.

Dr Kašpar in person presided at the trial of the six VONS members and pronounced the sentence.

A very well informed President of the Municipal Court. . . . In 1981, the state rewarded him for his good work by naming him Minister of Justice.

But let us go back to the window in the Bendas' apartment. To Dr Kamila Bendová, mother of five, sentenced to four years of widowhood

Details of previous photo: The police camera and cable leading from it to the office of the President of the Municipal Court, Dr Kašpar.

although her husband is alive. She is a mathematician by profession, a Catholic by conviction. Let us, at least in this book, have her joined by her husband, a Catholic philosopher who, out of love of his wife, went on to study *her* subject, mathematics, and who was now serving four years in prison.

There were times when I found it impossible to think of the exact sciences as being compatible with a belief in God. Then a certain astronomer and physicist (who also happened to be a Communist) spent a whole evening telling me about the grey areas of his scientific disciplines, about all the question-marks and improbabilities that lie in wait for the scientist who tries to reason out materialistic theories and hypotheses to their logical conclusion — and he managed to shake my hitherto firm views on the relationship between science and faith. But since my capacity for theoretical thought is limited, I had to have *material* proof that fire and water can, under certain circumstances, coexist in order to become completely converted.

This proof came in the shape of the Bendas, husband and wife, and of many other deeply religious Charter signatories.

Their existence and attitudes radically changed my superficial view of the world we live in. My certainties suddenly became very uncertain. I was forced to take a look at things from quite a different angle than I had been used to, and to ask questions. Of others and of myself.

Yet, we all need some certainties in this life. It says in the Bible that Adam and Eve lived happily in the Garden of Eden until they tasted the fruit of the Tree of Knowledge. End of paradise.

This story can also be interpreted so that knowledge which casts doubt on universally accepted truths, wrecks carefully constructed

Dr Kamila Bendová.

myths, exposes problems where everything had seemed crystal clear and transparent, forces us to seek, find, lose, and seek again — that such knowledge makes happiness impossible. *It makes life in paradise impossible.*

But what kind of paradise would it be — what kind of paradise *is* it — if it is built on ignorance and stupidity? I see that all around me in the people who take part in "manifestations" and processions, those who dutifully decorate their windows with little Czechoslovak and Soviet flags on every state and Party anniversary, who eagerly raise their hand every time Comrade Chairman asks "who is for?" I can see how, with their other hand, they, figuratively speaking, try

Dr Václav Benda.

to cover their eyes and ears so as not to see and hear the farce they are taking part in. In order at all costs to acquire at least a tiny bit of that sorry private paradise of theirs consisting of pork and dumplings and sauerkraut, a car, and a cottage in the country. (And even then it is not the consumer's paradise as it is known in the West, for there are long queues at the butchers with pork frequently unobtainable.)

It seems to me that a more accurate and truthful interpretation of that Biblical story was provided by the seventeenth-century Czech pedagogue, Jan Amos Komenský (Comenius) in the title of one of his books: *Labyrinth of the World and Paradise of the Heart.* I believe that true certainties in this life are much more likely to be found in the realisation that things and relationships are complex and not simple, in accepting this complexity, trying to understand it, and ordering one's life accordingly. In the paradise of the heart.

No, I have not found God. Unless to find God can also mean to realise that it is not the moulds into which even the simplest among us try to squeeze the chaos of the world around them that are important, but rather how each and every one of us demonstrates his humanity.

Or lack of it:

Women's prison at Opava, the place in which the Czech journalist Otka Bednářová spent long days and months.

I do not like, and usually distrust, the

Behind the wall of the Opava Prison: women prisoners at exercise.

obligatory paeans of praise celebrating people who happen to have become symbols of something or other. Bravery, hard work, self-sacrifice, strong will, love ... The man (or woman) concerned frequently disappears beneath all the high-flown words and celebratory speeches, which in the end turn him into a marble statue — cold and lifeless.

It is for this reason that I have hitherto not written a single line about Otka Bednářová; and I find it difficult to write about her even now. Because in her case I cannot see how I can dispense with big words.

Not that I think that Charter 77 needs any symbols or marble statues to look up to. But if one were required, Otka Bednářová would quite certainly be the leading candidate. The families of political prisoners, men and women who have been unjustly prosecuted, and dozens of others would readily speak about her.

I am not going to. I shall confine myself to quoting an excerpt from the record of the court proceedings of the Prague Municipal Court on 23 October 1979, when Otka was sentenced to three years' imprisonment.

Bednářová: I'm not going to make a long final speech, I can't speak as well as Václav Havel. However, since I was not allowed to do so at the beginning, I'd like to say a few words about my reasons for working in VONS. In the sixties I took part, in my capacity as a journalist, in the rehabilitation trials ...

Dr Kašpar, the presiding judge, immediately interrupts her: Keep to the point, Mrs Bednářová! This is of no interest to the court.

Bednářová: Nevertheless, I'd just like to say that I was there to witness everything going to pieces ...

Dr Kašpar: Mrs Bednářová, earlier you refused to testify and suddenly you want to tell us ...

Bednářová: I'm 52 years old and would like to make up somehow for that part of my life when I remained silent because I was young . . .

From this moment the presiding judge attempts to silence her, so that both speak at the same time.

Dr Kašpar: All this is quite irrelevant, Mrs Bednářová!

Bednářová: But the reason I joined VONS was that I realised how monstrous those trials and verdicts were, which resulted in executions. I have since then dedicated my life to trying to prevent anything like that happening again. I simply cannot act otherwise, no matter what it may cost me.

The presiding judge does not allow Otka Bednářová to finish her final speech.

The smiling woman behind the barred window is Otka Bednářová, more than a year after her exchange with Dr Kašpar during her trial.

The circumstances under which this and the following pictures were taken are so unusual that I'm going to let Ivan, who took them, do the talking:

Having been told by former inmates where to find the isolation ward for "politicals" in the

Journalist Otta Bednářová at the window of her cell.

women's prison at Opava, one Sunday afternoon I stood on the deserted pavement by the prison wall and shouted "Otka!" and then again "Bednářová!"

After a while a figure appeared at one of the windows on the top floor and waved to me. Quickly I aimed my lens at her and took several photos. Then the woman at the window started gesticulating furiously, and I understood that she wanted me to leave, afraid just as I was that one of the omnipresent StB men might appear at any moment and arrest me. It is an offence to take photographs of Czechoslovak prisons, and if the woman I had photographed was really Otka Bednářová, then I had committed a crime, no less.

At that distance, however, it was impossible to tell if it was Otka. It was only later at home, after I had developed the film and enlarged the pictures, that I could be certain: Yes, it was her, gazing out of the window of her cell and smiling.

She was smiling, partly because she is an optimist by nature and partly perhaps because she recognised the photographer down there in the street.

I badly wanted to take these pictures in order to help her sons and all those other people in Czechoslovakia and abroad who were waging a campaign for her release. This was based not so much on arguments about her innocence and that of all the VONS members, whose imprisonment was an act of contempt by the Czechoslovak authorities for the Helsinki Accords as well as for Czechoslovakia's own laws and the basic rules of decency – the campaign for the release of Otka Bednářová was mainly based on her serious condition. She was so gravely ill that she would not leave the prison alive if the regime insisted on her serving her full term.

And now I held in my hands photos showing her smiling behind bars.

I smuggled the pictures out of the country with strong misgivings. But, I said to myself, perhaps people will understand. Perhaps they will comprehend the feelings of a woman who has spent over a year in complete isolation, surrounded only by StB men, warders, and stool-pigeons and who all of a sudden sees someone she knows and likes, so that for a fleeting moment she forgets the life she is forced to lead and feels happy. And smiles.

Who knows, perhaps I over-estimated the ability of western newspaper readers to understand her situation. Three weeks before I left Czechoslovakia I was given a fascinating opportunity to photograph Otka once more, this time in the relative freedom of her apartment in Prague. Shortly after she was released, having had her sentence interrupted for reasons of health. This encounter was an experience I am not likely ever to forget. An experience which vindicated my snapshots of the smiling Otka behind the barred window in a way I would not have dared to imagine.

I took the lift up to the seventh floor of the apartment house. Otka came out to meet me, I embraced her . . . and was appalled. I remember her as she had been a year and a half ago and as she appears on the photo with the other nine arrested members of VONS: a smiling, attractive middle-aged woman. Standing in front of me now was an emaciated old lady.

I was born after the war and thus saw the men and women returning from Nazi concentration camps only in films. But now I was seeing one with my own eyes. Otka is 164 cm tall and eighteen months earlier had weighed 65 kg. Now she weighed 45 kg, the same weight as when she was 14 years old. Her face was grey and drawn, her large light blue eyes standing out as the only distinct feature. Yet this wreck of a human being was smiling. Laughing. Just as she smiled at me several

Otta Bednářová on the day of her release.

months ago in Opava prison.

She talked, the words tumbling out
uncontrollably. She was still experiencing the shock
of her unexpectedly acquired "freedom". I keep
pressing the release of my camera. . . but then I stop.
Otka has picked up a bracelet lying on the table and
is showing me that she doesn't have to wear it on her
wrist, the bracelet slides all the way up to her

shoulder. Normally, nothing can stop me taking
photographs, but now suddenly I can't.

The woman who was most probably saved from
dying in prison by the actions of Amnesty
International and thousands of decent people in
Czechoslovakia and abroad, talks and laughs.

Laughs.

Because laughter is a weapon of self-defence,

one of the few weapons accessible to the helpless and humiliated victims of lawlessness.

In September 1968, in the Post Hotel in Vienna, I met a well-known Czech photographer. During that night of 21 August, when Soviet tanks rumbled through the streets of Prague, he had recalled his experience as a Jewish prisoner in Auschwitz, took his wife, his cameras and the family dog and drove directly to Vienna. The dog was the worst affected by their flight — it went into a state of shock and took several days to recover.

This led us to consider how man can stand more suffering than beast, and we discussed the fraternal international assistance Czechoslovakia had received from her allies in the Warsaw Pact as well as my friend's sojourn at Auschwitz. He talked about the stories of Arnošt Lustig, who so eloquently described the fate of Jews in Nazi concentration camps.

"Arnošt is marvellous. Nowhere have I read a more accurate account of what we went through. And yet ... You know, something is missing. Lustig is dead serious. If I knew how to write, I'd produce an anti-Lustig book about the concentration camps, which would also include

The forcible eviction of writer Pavel Kohout from his Prague flat.

all the funny things we experienced. Do you find that incredible? Humour in the shadow of the ovens? Let me tell you, if it weren't for a bit of fun now and again, no one would have survived. No one."

I had cause to remember his words many times since. Both in prison and during many ordinary days of Charter 77.

It is difficult to keep your sense of humour when you are being evicted from your home. In 1978 the writer Pavel Kohout was forcibly evicted from his Prague apartment by the security police.

The flat was small and not particularly luxurious, but its location was quite exclusive: in Hradčany Square, directly opposite the gates to the first courtyard of Prague Castle. Its windows afforded a magnificent view of the city, but also a less magnificent one of the highest Soviet representatives on their way to visit the President, and of the grateful citizens who came on various occasions "spontaneously" to demonstrate their loyalty and love. StB men with short wave radios first took up positions all round the square and then the citizens of Prague were admitted, having been given paid leave from work for this purpose.

It was understandably intolerable that a Charter signatory should be in possession of such a splendid vantage point, and so one day the pantechnicons arrived in the square, StB men with short wave radios took up their positions (though the citizens of Prague did not get paid leave this time), and the house move went ahead.

Our photographer was the only civilian not working for the police in Hradčany Square at the time, which meant he had to take his pictures surreptitiously and without being able to focus his camera. This inevitably shows in the quality of the photos, but on the whole it seems to me that they express the right mood. Sad and sombre.

As if to compensate, he and the evicted writer put together a photo-story.

The photographs are really self-explanatory, but should anyone need a caption, I could not hope to improve on the text provided by the official representatives of the Czechoslovak regime of real socialism.

In 1978, Pavel Kohout was given permission to spend a year abroad, first to attend a ceremony at which he was awarded the Austrian State Prize for European Literature and then to travel in Europe and overseas. When, after less than twelve months, he drove back to his country, Czechoslovak frontier guards pushed his car back over the Austrian border, telling him that he must first go to the Czechoslovak Embassy in Vienna. There, he was informed that he had been deprived of his citizenship and would not be allowed to return home.

But now for something less serious.

One of the spokesmen of Charter 77, Professor Jiří Hájek, drove his secret police "shadows" to frenzy by his habit of leaving home each morning in his tracksuit and jogging, which involved a cross-country run of some seven kilometres and sometimes a dip in the nearby dam, even on cold autumn winter mornings.

Jiří Hájek was only following an old routine: when he was Czechoslovak Ambassador in London, he used to jog every morning on Hampstead Heath and round Kenwood, while during his time as Czechoslovak Ambassador to the UN he would regularly go running in Central Park.

His police "watchers" did not know all this and thought that he was just being difficult, trying to make their hard life even more onerous. But no matter how much they tried to persuade him,

Professor Hájek was not suddenly about to change the habit of a lifetime — and so one of the secret policemen had to get into *his* tracksuit every morning and plod dutifully along behind his quarry.

I really think I could not possibly conclude this brief look at the people of Charter 77 more fittingly than with this little anecdote about the daily routine of the former Czechoslovak Ambassador, Minister of Foreign Affairs, and one of the first three Charter spokesmen. Not so much because it has its humorous side but rather for the way it illustrates Professor Hájek's resolve to defend his right to act and live according to his own lights, despite all the efforts of the powers-that-be to make him conform. Not only in matters of principle but also in the little things which at first sight may not seem too important.

But only at first sight.

There is to this day in a Prague apartment an interesting book which the secret police have failed to discover, for all their house searches. It contains the statements of several hundred people giving their reasons for having signed Charter 77, a kind of sociological survey of great significance. Only about a fifth of those questioned specifically mentioned their interest in public affairs, in the struggle for human and civil rights, in the fate of their long-suffering country. In most cases, these political reasons are contained, so to speak, between the lines, as the inevitable consequence of their moral attitudes. The response of some eighty per cent of those asked can perhaps best be summed up in the words of one of them: "I signed the Charter because I would like to be able to look at myself in the mirror when I shave."

This, I believe, reflects the revulsion most people in Czechoslovakia feel towards Byzanti-

Pavel Kohout.

nism in general and Byzantinism in politics in particular. And it reflects their disillusionment with a great ideology that has come a cropper. "As soon as an idea becomes an ideology it is doomed to failure, because an idea cannot be universalised," wrote Friedrich Dürenmatt, and many Charter signatories felt he had spoken on their behalf.

But in a country in which literally everything is politicised — from an ice hockey match to the harvest, from the consumption of beer to Sunday outings — in a country in which political discrimination, hypocrisy and corruption are rife, the private attitudes of individuals automatically (and ironically) become political attitudes par excellence.

Charter 77 is an attempt to create a small island of normality in a raging sea of absurdity.

Or — if you want to look at it more pessimistically — it is an attempt to build a tiny garden on the busy crossroads of several motorways.

93

94

95

Professor *Jiří Hájek, former Czechoslovak Foreign Minister and Charter spokesman, on his regular morning jo*

A Pesso-optimistic
Conclusion

In the spring of 1980 I received a message from the Charter spokesmen, giving the latest figure for the number of signatories:

1,048.

One thousand and forty-eight men and women. In a country of fifteen million.

That is to say, Charter 77 was signed by less than one-tenth of one per cent of the population. If we were able to devote a photo to each signatory, we would end up with a picture book almost the size of the Oxford Illustrated Dictionary. However, in a public library containing volumes with pictures of all the fifteen million inhabitants of present-day Czechoslovakia our book would vanish like a drop in the ocean.

In Czechoslovakia, people walk in the street, play with their children, drive their cars or travel by train, visit shops and pubs and theatres, listen to the radio and television. To the casual visitor who comes here as a tourist, Prague may seem a little more drab than he or she had expected, the hotels somewhat inferior, the shops less well supplied with goods — but otherwise?

Nothing very terrible is happening here. Life may not be overly comfortable, but people lead ordinary lives, don't they?

So what about this famous Charter 77? Is it really anything more than a big bubble artificially inflated by imperialist propaganda — as we are constantly told by the propaganda of real socialism?

This question can best be answered by another:

If Charter 77 really represents only a negligible and unrepresentative handful of people, if their activity and their very existence is of no interest to anyone in Czechoslovakia, why do the official media, the secret police, the courts, and all the other organs of a totalitarian state go to such lengths to combat them?

But that would be a very inadequate reply, only partially illuminating the reality behind the question.

The famous Czech novelist Milan Kundera, who, like Pavel Kohout has been deprived of his Czechoslovak citizenship and has been living in France for the past 10 years, wrote a story while still living in Czechoslovakia in 1969, a story that has never been published there. I don't have a copy at hand and have forgotten its plot and denouement, but I well remember a monologue by its chief protagonist which I will quote as best I can:

"Let's say a man comes up to you and says — my dear sir, I am a fish. How are you to react? You, of course, realise that the man is a nut case. So are you to try and talk him out of it? If you say to him — oh come on, my dear fellow, you are

A Prague crowd.

Group of Charter 77 signatories.

Queuing for meat.

Prague grafitti (Havel is in jail — long may he live).

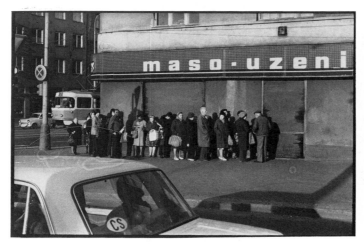

Statue of Klement Gottwald, first Communist President of Czechoslovakia.

not! Look, you don't have any fins! Nor any gills, so if I pushed you under water you'd drown — should you start arguing with him in this way, you would in effect be joining him in his lunacy. No, the only thing to do in such a case is to smile and say — but of course you are! And what a lovely fish, too! Just look at that splendid dorsal fin of yours, and the magnificent shine of your scales! You are the most beautiful fish I've ever laid eyes on. And then take your leave as fast as you can.''

My apologies to Milan Kundera for the very inaccurate quotation, but in his story he very accurately recorded the way the majority of Czechoslovakia's fifteen million citizens — those who did not sign Charter 77 — behave in the face of their lunatic rulers.

The trouble is that the man-fish they are confronted with is not merely some poor harmless loony. It is a madman who has soldiers, tanks, bombers, policemen and prisons at his beck and call. From someone like him you can't just take your leave, or not for any length of time. He demands to be told that he has a beautiful dorsal fin at least once a day, every day of the week, year in year out.

As a result, those who at first refuse to lower themselves to his level of lunacy become increasingly more schizophrenic, having of necessity to live a double life — a life of public supplication of those in power and a private one of contempt or indifference.

So how is one to reply to that simple question?

Perhaps as follows: There is every rational reason for people to conform — or at the very least to pretend to conform — with those in power in Czechoslovakia, who have every conceivable means of compulsion at their disposal.

Anyone who wishes to make a political career within the system must obviously not even think about signing the Charter.

Anyone who wishes to lead a quiet, relatively prosperous life, leaving political and civic affairs to officials of the regime who daily tell him, on TV and in the newspapers, that not only he but everyone else is a fish — must obviously not even think about signing the Charter.

However, if human beings since the beginning of time had belonged only to these two categories, man would to this day be living in the trees and walking on all fours, would never have invented the wheel and would woo his mate by hitting her over the head with a club and dragging her home by the hair. (Who knows, he might even in a certain sense be happier — ignorance being bliss — but that is another story.)

Throughout history there have always existed tiny groups of people known in English under the apt term of "outcasts". People belonging to a persecuted, and frequently despised, minority which played the same role in society as yeast in the making of bread. Don Quixotes who, to their

Double crucifixion.

Statue.

contemporaries, seemed ridiculous but have in retrospect come to be viewed as tragic heroes who helped to push mankind a little way forward.

I don't think it is an exaggeration to say that Charter 77 consists of just such people.

It may even be too modest a claim.

Charter 77 is a long-distance runner who covers his section of the relay with the almost unanimous approval of the fans crowding the full but silent stadium, a runner who has not only the distance and time and his own exhaustion to contend with but also the ill-will of the race organisers. They do their utmost to trip him up, try to chase him off the track, dig ditches and place barbed wire obstacles in his way. He is running the first, inhumanely long part of the race and has no one to whom he could hand over the baton. (The sprinters will only turn up when the finishing line is in sight.)

Maybe he won't finish the race, maybe he will collapse long before the end, and the sports journalists will write that he had chosen the wrong tactics, that he had overestimated his ability, that he had not trained enough. But always there will be someone to pick up the fallen baton and carry on...

Until he finishes the race.

Or collapses in his turn?

No, this is too morbid a conclusion. Nor is the sporting metaphor altogether fitting — a humble person appears to be a conceited elitist, and vice versa.

This book is intended to give testimony about ordinary people making their way in the dark, trying to light their own and others' path with a candle in an age of nuclear energy and space flights. That, I think, is a better way to describe the voluntary association that is Charter 77, calling for a return to common decency in a world of Potemkin villages with its decor of grandiose ideals and still more grandiose slogans behind which there is nothing but a black backdrop and a crumbling wall.

I have called this last part of the book a "pesso-optimistic" conclusion; let me briefly try to explain why.

It could not possibly have been just optimistic because, to quote an old saying, optimism usually denotes lack of information.

But nor could it be just pessimistic. Black despair in Czechoslovakia has been countered by the flickering candle of Charter 77, and even if this were the only source of light in that nocturnal gloom (which it is not), we would still have no right to be totally pessimistic. If nothing else, that would be a slap in the face of those men and women whose photographs grace this book. We would be denying their very existence. (And please understand, I am now speaking not only of the Charter signatories but also of those others whose faces you can see in this last section of the book. The conformists. The schizoids. The unhappy ones.)

I have no intention of indulging in futurology, to start discussing all the changes in foreign and domestic policy that must take place before people in Czechoslovakia can hope to lead a decent, human existence. Partly because all theory is grey whereas life is full of colour, but also because for all our isolation we have not lost our sense of proportion — neither I nor, in particular, those people in Czechoslovakia who belong to Charter 77.

Which is why we still compare the nightmare of Czechoslovakia with the even greater nightmares of the Soviet Union and Chile, Cambodia and Cuba, Paraguay, South Africa, Afghanistan...

The twentieth century has provided us with many a reason to give way to blackest depair, when this may indeed have seemed the easiest way out: in 1914, 1929, 1933, 1938, 1939, 1948, 1956, 1968... as well as today. And these are just a few dates relevant to Central Europe — every country in the world can come up with others of its own.

But time has one outstanding (though from the individual's point of view horrific) characteristic: it never stops, not even for a moment. The years pass, the seasons come and go.

Despite changes in the climate, winter is always followed by spring — at least in our northern hemisphere.

And so there can be no doubt that a Prague spring will again follow the present long Prague winter.

When?

If only I knew that, if anyone knew the answer to this simple question, I would not have to call this part of our book a "pesso-optimistic" conclusion.

Charter 77.

P.S.

This book was born in Prague in 1980. It was first published in 1983 in Swedish in Stockholm, because it was only then that both its authors found themselves in emigration abroad. Now comes an English edition — the original Czech version may or may not be published later.

A great deal has happened to the people whose faces you saw in the photographs, many of them have had quite dramatic experiences since 1980, but after due reflection we decided against trying to bring the text up to date. The book was intended to present a photographic document of its time, and the last picture in it was taken in 1980.

We have allowed ourselves only two exceptions to this general rule, both of them in extreme cases: with feelings of bitter irony we have added two sentences about the meteoric rise of the President of the Prague Municipal Court, Dr Kašpar, and with much pleasure we recorded that one of the Charter signatories, the poet Jaroslav Seifert, had won the 1984 Nobel Prize for Literature.

All that remains to be said by way of a postscript is that the secret police has still not succeeded in liquidating Charter 77, which in January 1985 celebrated its eighth birthday. This despite the fact that the methods used by the authorities have been "perfected" and the persecution intensified. The Charter movement continues to exist and work. It is part of Czechoslovakia's history — and of its present.

London, February 1985.

Karel Kyncl in front of the Bory Prison in Pilsen, where he spent 10 months.